Gaillard

in

Deaf America

Gaillard in Deaf America

A PORTRAIT OF THE DEAF COMMUNITY, 1917

Henri Gaillard

Bob Buchanan, Editor
Translated by William Sayers

Gallaudet University Press
Washington, D.C.

Gallaudet Classics in Deaf Studies
A Series Edited by John Vickrey Van Cleve

Gallaudet University Press
Washington, DC 20002

The photographs on pages 4, 27, 74, 109, and 117 appear courtesy
of the Gallaudet University Archives. The photograph on page 9 is
courtesy of the Pennsylvania Society for the Advancement of the
Deaf, Inc.

Library of Congress Cataloging in Publication Data

Gaillard, Henri, 1866–
   [Mission de sourds-muets francais aux Etats-Unis. English]
   Gaillard in deaf America : a portrait of the deaf community,
   1917/Henri Galliard ;
Robert Buchanan, editor ; translated by William Sayers.
   p. ; cm.
Includes bibliographical references.
ISBN 1–56368–122–6 (alk. paper)
   1. Deaf—United States. 2. Deaf—United States—Social
conditions. I. Buchanan, Robert (Robert M.) II. Title.

HV2545 .G35513 2002

362.4'22'097309041—dc21   2002019732

CONTENTS

INTRODUCTION
Bob Buchanan

Our understanding of the culture, contributions, and history of this nation's deaf community has grown greatly over the past thirty years. This is due in no small measure to an increasingly varied collection of popular as well as academic works in fiction and nonfiction. Many of these books have chronicled the origins and growth of the deaf community during the late nineteenth century or depicted contemporary issues in areas such as education, the arts, and public life. These efforts have enriched deaf studies, broadened the emerging field of disability history, and helped us better understand the distinctive and common experiences of this country's diverse communities of citizens.[1]

Amid these academic and popular advances, however, works by deaf authors that have surveyed the deaf community and American society at large have been extremely uncommon. *Gaillard in Deaf America* is just such a welcomed exception. In it, Henri Gaillard, a French deaf activist and leader, offers an engaging account of his travels to the United States during the summer of 1917 that is certain to delight and inform readers interested in the deaf community and mainstream society.

1

An adroit writer with a sharp memory, a perceptive eye, and an engaging personality, Gaillard composed an insightful journal that recounts his visit with the American deaf community. For three months, Gaillard, accompanied by French colleagues Jean Olivier, Edmond Pilet, and Eugene Graff, traveled up and down the east coast and into the Midwest.[2] They visited schools and colleges, social clubs and conventions, private residences and workplaces, meeting both deaf leaders and ordinary adults. Beginning in Hartford, Gaillard and company traveled to metropolitan New York, Buffalo, Akron, Pittsburgh, Philadelphia, and Washington D.C., where they were welcomed by their deaf colleagues.

Gaillard was more than an astute chronicler of the deaf community; he was also a perceptive student of American culture and life. Although he was most intent on conveying the ideas and institutions of the deaf community, his account also brims with engaging sketches of the wider world. The careful reader will not help but notice that some of his portrayals, while representative of the early twentieth century, are now understood to be inaccurate, and even troubling. His stereotypical representation of Jews as frugal business leaders comes to mind, as does his frequent depiction of Germans as "Huns." Beyond these shortcomings, however, Gaillard also deftly draws the reader into the perils and delights of rural and urban life in the formative years of the past century. Whether worrying about the dangers of automobiles that careen about at the dizzying speed of sixty miles per hour, marveling at dazzling new skyscrapers, or decrying the decline of once pristine rivers now darkened by industrial soot, Gaillard remains an accomplished and inviting storyteller. This is his journal.

The impetus for Gaillard's visit began not in France but the United States. In the fall of 1916, Jay Cook Howard, the eighth president of the National Association of the Deaf (NAD), eagerly invited representatives of the "deaf of France" to journey to Hartford, Connecticut, the following summer to celebrate the 100th anniversary of the American School for the Deaf (ASD), the first permanent school for deaf students in the United States.[3]

French and American deaf citizens, Howard understood, shared a common history. In the United States, ASD's centennial symbolized a century of educational and cultural progress for deaf citizens. In France, deaf citizens took special pride in the advanced status and education of American deaf adults. One century before, France's brilliant deaf teacher Laurent Clerc, gave up a teaching career in Paris and sailed to the United States, where he assisted the Reverend Thomas Hopkins Gallaudet, an eager but inexperienced evangelical, in founding ASD. Over the next forty years, they worked with unparalleled success to establish and expand the impact of the venerable institution. In their efforts, these men advanced forever the standing of America's deaf citizens.[4]

France's Henri Gaillard, the recipient of Howard's invitation, also understood this vital legacy. Having come of age during France's Third Republic, with its progressive emphasis on universal suffrage for men and the rights of man, he had worked steadily to advance the position of the country's marginalized deaf citizens. Born in 1866 and deafened by an explosion at age five, he attended schools for hearing students, later transferring to the National Institute for the Deaf in Paris. By age twenty he was a skilled printer, and by twenty-seven he was editor of the *Gazette des Sourds-Muets*, or *Deaf Gazette*, the nation's only independent newspaper by and about France's deaf community. Troubled that the vast majority of France's deaf adults had no access to advanced schooling and often faced discrimination by employers, Gaillard had worked to improve conditions for his peers. In an era when few leaders, deaf or hearing, had the opportunity to travel, Gaillard had journeyed widely as a representative for French deaf adults. Prior to 1900, he attended and delivered papers at some half dozen international convocations in the United States and Europe.[5]

If historical trends guaranteed French enthusiasm for the NAD's invitation, securing funds for the proposed journey

[handwritten margin note: Gaillard growing up, his deaf story + contribution to deaf community]

Henri Gaillard

depended upon gaining support from both deaf and hearing citizens—no simple undertaking for the dispersed deaf community.
By April 1917, Gaillard and others based in Paris had organized
a committee to raise money and select a group to make the
transatlantic crossing. The group circulated a letter throughout
Paris's deaf community that emphasized the journey's historic significance, underscoring the "duty" of the French deaf to sustain

Clerc's tradition of activity, which had brought "intellectual liberation to the deaf of the whole world."

Ongoing concern regarding the educational status of French deaf students impelled other deaf adults to lend a hand. In particular, "oralist" French educators, by the early twentieth century, had broken with the longstanding tradition of sign-based education advocated by Clerc and others.[6] Instead, these hearing administrators had moved to minimize if not eliminate sign language in favor of methods that emphasized articulation and lipreading. Angry French deaf adults countered that these changes imperiled the education and vocational standing of students. Instead, most, including Gaillard, promoted "combined" practices that supported both sign language and oral training. Gaillard and his peers understood that a visit to the United States would be a timely opportunity to galvanize transatlantic opposition to "pure" oralism.

For some in the French and American deaf communities, the trip also provided an opportunity to champion their patriotism. The United States had entered World War I as an ally of France weeks prior to Gaillard's departure. Deaf men in the United States and France, typically blocked from serving as soldiers, sought alternate opportunities to demonstrate their patriotism and "manhood."[7] For these men (and some women as well), Gaillard and company functioned as unofficial ambassadors whose travels symbolized the earnestness and involvement of the larger deaf community. As the date of ASD's centennial fast approached, deaf citizens from Paris and across the country donated francs while anxious deaf leaders petitioned civic and governmental agencies and leaders outside the deaf community. By the spring of 1917, with little time to spare, they had gathered sufficient resources.

Eager to begin their journey, Gaillard's party assembled on the French coast. Just prior to sailing, the group briefly toured the schools for deaf girls and boys at rue Saint-Sernin and rue de Marseille. Their visit underscored the educational divisions confronting deaf adults that would be evident throughout their journey to the United States. After visiting one class, Gaillard

acknowledged the oral training of several students but noted that
a longer visit would have enabled him to "find the little rebels
against the pure oral method." On the 23d of June, the group
set sail for the United States.

   As the account will show, in the United States Gaillard found
a proud but embattled minority community. Deaf citizens her-
alded their individual and collective educational, vocational and
cultural accomplishments, for many made possible by the founding of ASD. In one century, thousands of deaf children and adults
had received vocational and academic instruction, either at ASD
or other private and public institutions across the continent
inspired by ASD's methods and accomplishments. Hundreds
more had gone on to advanced studies, often at Gallaudet College, at the time the world's only college for deaf and hard of
hearing students. Whatever their particular background or training, the nation's deaf adults had earned acclaim as farmers, arti-
sans, entrepreneurs, artists and more. In short, in this pivotal
century deaf adults had constructed a unique national community with its own visual language, schools, and organizations.
   Gaillard's narrative account also provides compelling evidence that deaf citizens, like other minorities in the early twentieth century, were at risk. Acclaimed for its representative
democracy, its growing industrial might and its entrepreneurial
genius, the United States in the early twentieth century was also
a segregated country defined by hierarchy and division. In its
rapid and often discordant transformation from a scattering of
colonies to an industrial giant that spanned the continent and
beyond, the national culture and civil society privileged white
over black and red, men over women, the affluent over the
impoverished, the "able-bodied" over the "disabled," and, of
course, the hearing over the deaf.
   In particular, from the 1870s through the early twentieth
century, the nation's deaf citizens found themselves enmeshed
in an epic struggle over their identity and future. During this piv-

otal period, an influential corps of hearing professionals and parents of deaf children, drawn by the appealing vision that deaf children could be *restored* to mainstream society by learning how to speak and understand spoken language, advocated a series of sweeping educational, civil and social changes.[8] These conflicts were centered in the nation's private and public schools.[9] Sign language, the predominant means of communication at ASD, had been broadly acclaimed and widely used by deaf and hearing educators for much of the nineteenth century. By the latter part of the century, however, sign language had come under fire and its use greatly reduced or prohibited in schools.

By the early twentieth century, oral approaches that favoured articulation and lip reading had become predominant. In 1887, out of some 8,000 students, almost 5,500 were educated by the *combined* approach that featured sign language but included oral training for students that demonstrated an aptitude.[10] By 1915, however, the majority of the nation's deaf students were instructed, not in sign language, but through writing and oral methods: among some 13,000 students, nearly 9,000 were guided by oral approaches.[11]

[margin note: deaf education timeline]

These changes transformed not only instruction but also instructors. Deaf teachers, long respected by students for their skills, insight and commitment, came under increasing pressure from hearing administrators to step away from the academic classrooms many had helped build.[12] The number of deaf instructors peaked in the 1870s, at approximately 250 of 550 teachers and administrators—roughly 40 percent of the instructional force. Yet by 1918, out of some 1,850 academic teachers, only 270, or less than 20 percent, were deaf.[13]

As hearing educators sought to *restore* deaf students to the hearing world, like-minded professionals in mainstream society also questioned the very standing of the emergent deaf community. Respected hearing educators and civic leaders led by the brilliant and influential Alexander Graham Bell implored deaf adults not to inter-marry or at least remain childless—lest they bear deaf children.[14] Indeed, Edward Miner Gallaudet, president of Gallaudet

[margin note: marriage / children of deaf adults]

College and son of Thomas Hopkins Gallaudet, publicly questioned not only the usefulness of sign language but encouraged deaf adults to limit their involvement with the community's rich repertoire of social and cultural organizations, for fear they'd be seen as "clannish," not properly integrated into mainstream society.[15] In these ways and others, the cultural, linguistic, and educational underpinnings, indeed the very legitimacy, of the emergent deaf community itself had become contested.

Optimistic in character and content, Gaillard's journal ably conveys these historical conflicts; it also offers an extended portrait of a rich and vibrant extended community of deaf individuals and families. His visits to schools for deaf students, for example, while snapshots rather than extended studies, reflect this dualism. In Gaillard's description of ASD and its leaders, the reader will find a historic sensitivity and a tone of reverence most often associated with visits to churches and religious leaders. This admiration is not without foundation. As Gaillard notes, the school served as an incubator for the national deaf community. By 1893, for example, more than 2,500 children and adults had received sign-based instruction at Hartford. At a national level, ASD's success also hastened the efforts of other deaf and hearing citizens who favored the establishment of schools. By mid-century, schools had been organized in seventeen states; by century's end, the establishment of schools had become a national norm. At the same time, by 1917, ASD, like most other schools across the country, had undergone a significant transformation. Oral instruction was predominant, with oral classes eclipsing manual classes by sixteen to three.[16]

Gaillard's brief visit and favorable sketches of the Pennsylvania Institution for the Deaf in the Mt. Airy section of Philadelphia, give little evidence of the school's significance in these changes. Founded in 1820 and briefly led by Clerc, the Pennsylvania school provided instruction in sign language for its first half century. In 1892, however, the Mt. Airy campus earned national notice. Under the direc-

*The French delegation to the American School for the Deaf's
one-hundred-year anniversary celebration*

[handwritten margin note: division of schools: - pure oral - oral failures]

tion of Albert Crouter, the school was physically divided into two distinct camps: the first for the majority of students to be taught in a pure oral environment; the second for "oral failures," to be instructed in sign language. By 1899, ninety percent of students were raised in an all-oral environment. Sign language, Crouter declared, was an unnecessary and unwanted reminder of a past era.[17]

Not surprisingly, deaf educators and leaders in Pennsylvania and across the country challenged Crouter's claims. In one critique, several advocates charged that students who did not acquire oral skills were often mislabeled "feeble-minded" and improperly dismissed. Without the power to investigate the school, these critics were unable to alter the practices they decried. While these conflicts at Mt. Airy were not in evidence at the time of his visit, Gaillard's journal indicates that deaf leaders remained steadfast in their opposition to oralist practices.

Gaillard's extended discussion of the founding and early history of the New York Institution for the Deaf in New York City, affectionately known as Fanwood (after the location of its campus), is instructive in several respects. Under the tutelage of Edward Hodgson, an accomplished editor, typography instructor and respected national leader, students printed the *Deaf Mute's Journal (DMJ)*, for decades a definitive source of news and commentary regarding the national deaf community.[18] Moreover, as oral instruction displaced deaf teachers from the academic classroom, many were able to retain employment in vocational departments where they remained skilled mentors to students. None were more influential than Hodgson.

[margin note: deaf teachers → but deaf Mentors]

[margin note: No deaf teachers → but deaf Mentors]

The contemporary reader may also be intrigued by the school's emphasis on military dress and culture, especially for its boys. In addition to providing effective academic and vocational instruction, deaf and hearing teachers and administrators sought to shape the moral character of their charges. A far cry from today's informal dress and personalized approach, this stress on standardized appearance and bearing was intended to remind youngsters of the ongoing responsibilities they faced as adult representatives of the small and embattled deaf community. As Hodgson explained in a representative *DMJ* editorial, "No deaf man lives for himself alone."[19]

Apart from ASD, Gallaudet College may have been most significant to the national deaf community. While the contemporary visitor to Gallaudet University will find a vibrant campus that draws several thousand deaf and hearing undergraduate and graduate students from across the globe, the modest institution of this earlier era brought together some one hundred students, primarily in the liberal arts and education. Gaillard's glowing portrait of the college, then fifty years old, is consistent with his veneration for ASD. If the American School was the birthplace of deaf education, Gallaudet College was its zenith.

The deaf community, as Gaillard's account demonstrates, featured a rich array of local, regional, and national groups and organizations. In one of his visits to metropolitan New York, for example, Gaillard mentions at least eight separate social and civic clubs. In fact, these groups emerged from ASD's success. As deaf students across the nation lived and studied together at residential schools, many graduates sought to sustain and enlarge these relationships into adulthood. By the late nineteenth century, deaf adults had organized a host of school-based as well as local, state and national organizations. As Henry Rider, a leader of New York's deaf community, explained in 1877, these organizations served an indispensable social purpose, that of enabling adults otherwise dispersed across the continent to satisfy a "longing desire and almost irresistible impulse" to communicate and socialize.[20] Gaillard confirms these sentiments in a host of accounts: from evening festivities in New York's Coney Island, to afternoon picnics at Hartford's idyllic Lake Compounce, to dinner parties among friends, deaf adults came together to share and celebrate their diverse and shared experiences.

[handwritten margin note: formed by deaf students who lived + studied in residential schools]

If an urge to socialize was the driving force behind some organizations, external conditions, both troubling and favorable, spurred the growth of still other groups. Gaillard's discussion of the National Fraternal Society of the Deaf (Frat) is a case in point. While the reader may be drawn to the author's vivid description of the hazing rites imposed upon Frat initiates, the organization's more staid history bears review. Currently a thriving organization with seven thousand members, the Frat, first incorporated in 1901, has provided insurance and support to its members who were typically denied services by mainstream organizations. By the time of Gaillard's visit, an extraordinary 3,000 members were organized into more than sixty local groups. Equally important, in its first decade of existence, the Frat provided much needed benefits to hundreds of deaf families, many of them financially needy.

Less renowned than the Frat but no less remarkable was the Communal Center for the Jewish Deaf in New York City. The center was noteworthy because it exemplified a pattern of providing educational and vocational assistance to individual deaf workers, especially the most vulnerable. In his efforts to secure

work for unemployed adults, Employment Bureau Director
Albert Amateau followed longstanding approaches of the deaf
community. A hearing man, Amateau, like many deaf leaders,
openly frowned on charity and instead sought to educate reluc-
tant or ignorant employers about the skills of deaf prospects. He
compared his role to that of a sign language interpreter: "We are
simply interpreters for the deaf in the same sense one would be
an interpreter for men speaking a foreign tongue."[21] Moreover,
as Gaillard notes, the center's deaf and hearing administrators
were effective. Between 1913 and the close of World War I, the
center secured employment for up to two hundred adults each
year.[22]

Among the varied institutions visited by Gaillard, none were
more significant than churches. Over the span of his visit, he frequented several of the most successful, including New York's St.
Ann's Church founded by Thomas Gallaudet Jr. in 1872 and
Philadelphia's All Soul's Church founded in 1888 and ably led
by the country's first ordained deaf pastor, Henry Syle.[23] As deaf
adults pooled in urban areas or close to residential schools, many
sought not only fellow deaf congregants but spiritual support and
guidance. In fact, by the early twentieth century, several dozen
churches, typically Episcopalian or Protestant and often led by
deaf clergy, served predominantly deaf congregations. In addition to religious sustenance these institutions also provided charitable assistance, vocational guidance, and a gathering place for
individuals and families alike.

No organization visited by Gaillard more aptly illustrates the
accomplishments of and dangers before deaf adults than the
National Association of the Deaf (NAD). Established in 1880,
the NAD of 1917, like the larger deaf community, was proud
and also beleaguered. At once a celebration of individual accomplishment and deaf culture, the NAD was also a forum for leaders to hold forth on the educational, vocational, civic, and cultural
challenges confronting deaf citizens.[24]

Gaillard arrived in Hartford after the NAD convention had
begun, and his hurried notes reflect his rushed attendance at a

wide mix of meetings and presentations. Certainly, his late arrival did not dampen the warm reception he received. NAD President Jay Cooke Howard brought Gaillard and company to the stage of Hartford High's auditorium to stand before the eight hundred deaf adults then in attendance. As Gaillard described the reception, "the huge hall was filled with a sea of handkerchiefs and waving hands as a joyful sign of welcome." After giving brief introductory presentations, Gaillard, Pilet, Graff, and Olivier were named honorary members of the NAD.

These conventions, typically held every three years, can be seen as portraits that illustrate the state of mind of deaf leaders. With their evenings marked by celebratory banquets and stirring toasts delivered in sign language, the days were also filled with an array of committee meetings, debates and often impassioned presentations regarding the issues of the day. Not surprisingly, several presentations at the 1917 meeting focused on the ongoing methods debate. The appendix includes a powerful and poignant condemnation of educational practices by New York's senior statesman Edward Hodgson who regularly advocated on behalf of sign language throughout his illustrious career.

NAD leaders also sought to influence public policy. At the close of each convention, for example, leaders composed resolutions summarizing their concerns. Hartford's declarations were representative and included unequivocal support for sign language; backing for oral instruction, but only "for those deaf who can profit by it;" and endorsement of an International Confederation of the Deaf that would promote combined approaches in instruction.[25] While these resolutions did not measurably influence events at that time, they have remained as steadfast positions advanced with increasing effectiveness by generations of deaf leaders over the course of the century.

Gaillard's account also illustrates that the deaf community was enriched by its tradition of honouring the contributions and service of past leaders and elders, deaf and hearing alike.

Although his discussions of Laurent Clerc are scattered rather than substantive, Clerc's overarching influence is undeniable. Similarly, the author's sensitive account of his brief visit to a frail Edward Miner Gallaudet, the first leader of Gallaudet College, is affecting.[26] Finally, his moving descriptions of several homes for aged and infirm deaf adults are heartening reflections of the wider community's uncommon commitment to the health and well being of its elders.

An additional contribution of the journal is the collective portrait of individual accomplishments. Gaillard visited some half dozen cities where he conferred and socialized with a representative mix of male deaf leaders from fields as varied as education, industry, and small businesses, as well as the arts and sciences.[27] While one can wish that the author had also deemed it instructive to record his thoughts on the contributions of the women he encountered, the profiles of male leaders he offers remain noteworthy.[28]

Several characteristics unite these leaders and may be a key to their success. All were uncommonly skilled and committed— certainly effective counterpoints to the systemic barriers of discrimination and ignorance that were commonplace in the early twentieth century. Moreover, the majority had access to advanced academic or vocational instruction, including attendance at Gallaudet College. The NAD, for example, has often been dubbed the "Gallaudet Club" because most of its leaders attended the school. Overall, this combination of drive, ability, and superior academic or vocational training was determinative in enabling these men to achieve not merely success, but prominence in a wide range of fields.

At the same time, however, it bears noting that this remarkable leadership class was not representative of the broader national deaf community. Like other minority groups, the deaf community was divided by gender, racial, educational, and, of course, economic divisions. The reader may hunger for a more diverse portrait, one that could provide additional insight into the problems and pursuits of the deaf working women and men unable to attend the grand balls or exclusive restaurants fre- *more oppressed groups excluded within deaf community* quented by Gaillard and company. At the same time, the author's report on Akron's "Deaf Colony" of some 500 industrial work- men and women employed by the Goodyear Corporation pro- vides welcomed glimpses of these industrious individuals and their vibrant community.[29]

Moreover, if sustained academic and vocational instruction, more than any other factor, advanced the status of deaf adults, it should be noted that most children and adults received lit- tle more than primary or "elementary" instruction (typically over a period of five to ten years). Only a tiny minority ever acquired either the training or opportunity to attend Gallaudet College. By the 1920s, for example, it was estimated that ninety percent of the nation's deaf children received at least elemen- tary schooling. At the same time, these observers estimated that a majority of these students left school before they completed their education.[30] Overall, the experiences of the majority of ordinary deaf children and adults have been difficult to fully reconstruct.

Ultimately, this journal, like its author, is promising. On the one hand, the extraordinary leaders Gaillard profiles were excep- tional rather than numerous. On the other hand, the composite individual and collective history encompassed within this jour- nal represents a remarkable pattern of individual and collective determination and accomplishment—typically, in the face of daunting conditions. This enduring legacy of achievement is sure to inform and hearten contemporary readers as they consider the challenges and opportunities before the deaf community and the nation at the onset of the twenty-first century.

Notes

1. My appreciation to Ivey Pittle Wallace and John Van Cleve for their support and incisive editorial suggestions. My thanks to Susan Burch at Gal- laudet University for her helpful reading and to Anne Quartararo at the United States Naval Academy for her references regarding Gaillard. As always, Michael

Olson at the Gallaudet University Archives provided prompt and thorough assistance.

2. Jean Olivier was the secretary general of the Fraternal Association of the Deaf of Champagne; Edmond Pilet was the secretary general of the National Union of the French Associations of the Deaf; and Eugene Graff was president of the Paris Deaf Center.

3. For information on Howard, see Wesley Lauritsen, "The Minnesota School for the Deaf," 1963, Gallaudet University Archives Vertical File (hereafter GUAVF); [eulogy] "J.C. Howard," *The Companion* (February 1946): 10; J. Schuyler Long, "The Deaf in Business: J. Cooke Howard Financier," *Silent Worker* (June 1901):145–46; James E. Gallaher, ed., *Representative Deaf Persons of the United States* (Chicago: James E. Gallaher, 1898), 112–14.

4. Clerc was born in La Balme, France, in December 1785. He first attended school at age twelve, where he studied with Superintendent Abbé Sicard. By twenty-one he was appointed as a teacher and ten years later, at age thirty-one, he met Thomas Gallaudet and agreed to leave for the United States. He died in Hartford at the age of eighty-three, after an unparalleled career as an esteemed intellectual, teacher, administrator, and role model. For biographical information begin with Harlan Lane's sweeping overview in *When the Mind Hears* (New York: Random House, 1984), Part one passim. A brief but helpful account is available in John Van Cleve and Barry Crouch, *A Place of Their Own* (Washington, D.C.: Gallaudet University Press, 1989), 37–45. Finally, an indispensable source is Clerc's own biographical account. See Laurent Clerc, "Laurent Clerc" in *Tribute to Gallaudet: A Discourse in Commemoration of the Life, Character and Services of the Reverend Thomas H. Gallaudet L.L.D.*, ed. Henry Barnard (Hartford, Conn.: Brockett & Hutchinson, 1852), 106–16.

This volume also contains useful information regarding Thomas Gallaudet. In addition, consult, Edward Miner Gallaudet, *Life of Thomas Hopkins Gallaudet: Founder of Deaf-Mute Instruction in America* (New York: Henry Holt, 1888); Heman Humphrey, *The Life and Labors of the Reverend T. H. Gallaudet* (New York: Robert Carter & Brothers, 1857).

5. For biographical information on Gaillard, begin with Anne Quartararo, "Republicanism, Deaf Identity, and the Career of Henri Gaillard in Late-Nineteenth-Century France," in *Deaf History Unveiled: Interpretations from the New Scholarship*, ed. John Van Cleve (Washington, D.C.: Gallaudet University Press, 1993), 40–52. See also, M. Prévost, Roman d'Amat H. Tribout de Morembert et JP Lobies, *Dictionnaire de Biographie Française* (Paris: Librairie Letouzey et Ane, 1980), 85.

6. For a brief but helpful historical discussion of efforts to educate deaf students, first in Europe and then the United States, begin with Van Cleve and Crouch, *A Place of Their Own*, 1–28.

7. Within the American deaf community, for example, deaf men and women donated funds through the NAD that were used to provide two ambulances for France. In addition, deaf adults also collaborated with their hearing peers at the local level to contribute to various war drives. See Robert Buchanan, *Illusions of Equality: Deaf Americans in School and Factory, 1850–1950* (Washington, D.C.: Gallaudet University Press, 1999), 73.

8. On instruction at the Hartford school, see Job Williams, *A Brief History of the American Asylum at Hartford for the Education and Instruction of the Deaf and Dumb* (Hartford, Conn.: Case, Lockwood and Brainard, 1893).

9. For the definitive narrative account of the development of schooling in the nineteenth century through 1918, see John W. Jones, "One Hundred Years of History in the Education of the Deaf in America and Its Present Status," *American Annals of the Deaf* 63 (January 1918): 1–47 passim. On trends at the turn of the century, see Edward Allen Fay, "Progress of Speech Teaching in the United States," *American Annals of the Deaf* 60 (January 1915): 115. For a compelling interpretive account that locates these trends in the context of intellectual and cultural shifts in the United States, begin with Douglas Baynton, *Forbidden Signs: American Culture and the Campaign against Sign Language* (Chicago: University of Chicago Press, 1996).

10. Jones, "One Hundred Years," 181–92. Research indicates that the 1870s were a pivotal decade for oralist approaches.

11. Fay, "Progress of Speech Teaching," 115.

12. Some two dozen deaf adults, many graduates of ASD, were instrumental in founding many of the nation's public schools, especially during the latter half of the nineteenth century. See, for example, Jack R. Gannon, *Deaf Heritage: A Narrative History of Deaf America* (Silver Spring, Md.: National Association of the Deaf, 1981), 18; Guilbert C. Braddock, *Notable Deaf Persons* (Washington, D.C.: Gallaudet College Alumni Association, 1975), 150–51; Edmund Boatner, "Deaf Teachers of the Deaf," *Silent Worker*, in vertical files: "Deaf Education," GUAVF.

13. Jones, "One Hundred Years," 7, 10–13.

14. For an astute analysis of Bell and the varied positions he so brilliantly espoused, begin with Baynton, *Forbidden Signs*, 30–31.

15. For a representative paper, see Edward Miner Gallaudet, "The Intermarriage of the Deaf and Their Education" *Science* 26 (8 November, 1890): 295–99.

16. On the ASD, see Job Williams, "The American Asylum," in *Histories of American Schools for the Deaf*, 1817–1893, vol.1, ed. Edward A. Fay, (Washington D.C.: Volta Bureau, 1893). Regarding the number of states and schools, see Jones, "One Hundred Years," 181–92.

17. Albert L. Crouter, "Changes of Method in the Pennsylvania Institution," *American Annals of the Deaf* 46 (January 1901): 62–68.

18. Born in England in 1854, and a typesetter by training, Hodgson was deafened at age eighteen and hired as an instructor at Fanwood when he was twenty-two. From 1878 through 1933 he edited the venerable *Deaf Mute's Journal*, arguably the deaf community's most influential newspaper. On Hodgson, see "Hodgson, E.A., Editor," in Gallaher, *Representative Deaf Persons*, 159–61; "Editor Hodgson," *Deaf Mute's Journal* (24 August , 1933): 2.

19. Editorial, *Deaf Mute's Journal* (9 November, 1905): 2.

20. "Elmira Convention of Deaf Mutes," *American Annals of the Deaf* 22 (October 1877): 251–52.

21. See Albert J. Amateau, "Details of Employment Bureau Work," *Proceedings of the Twentieth Convention of American Instructors of the Deaf* (Washington, D.C.: Government Printing Office, 1915): 63. See also pages 62–66.

22. "Sixth Annual Report—Year of 1917," *Jewish Deaf* (February 1918): 45–49; "Eighth Annual Report—Year of 1919," *Jewish Deaf* (February 1920): 50–73.

23. On these and other churches, see Otto Berg, *A Missionary Chronicle, Being a History of the Ministry to the Deaf in the Episcopal Church*, 1850–1980 (Hollywood, Md.: St. Mary's Press, 1984).

24. Women were active participants in the founding of state and national organizations but were generally excluded from positions of recognized leadership. Thirteen women joined sixty-eight men at the founding of the NAD. Only males were selected for leadership roles. See "Proceedings of the First National Convention of Deaf-Mutes," [Pamphlet] (New York: New York Institution for the Deaf and Dumb, 1880), 41–43.

25. Deaf leaders opposed uniform oral instruction for all students—not oral communication itself. Many deaf leaders of the era were late-deafened and regularly used their voices in communication with hearing adults.

26. Edward Miner Gallaudet died in September 1917, three months after Gaillard's visit. He was eighty-one.

27. Not unexpectedly, Gaillard makes little mention of the racial divide that defined not only the deaf community but also the nation at that time. After all, formal segregation was the law of the land and widely reinforced in American society and culture. While we know today that African Americans and their allies regularly resisted segregation, broad disavowal of *Jim Crow* would not come till the latter part of the century—and then, only grudgingly.

28. On the efforts of women to enlarge their standing in state and national organizations see, Robert Buchanan, *Deaf Students and Workers in the United States, 1800–1950* (Ph.D. diss., University of Wisconsin-Madison, 1995).

29. The Goodyear Corporation was but one of several industrial employers that actively recruited deaf workers during the World War I era. In Ohio and elsewhere across the nation, not only during this era but also again during World War II, employers opened their doors to groups of workers previously shunned, including women, African Americans and other workers of color as well as deaf and disabled individuals. For reference see Buchanan, *Illusions of Equality*, 69–85.

30. Harry Best, *Deafness and the Deaf in the United States* (New York: Macmillan, 1943), 192, 508. Best cited data from the 1910 and 1920 census indicating that 88.6 percent of white school-aged children attended school. Among African American children, however, the figure dropped to 63.9 percent—and that is likely optimistic. Overall, few private or public schools reported consistent, dependable data regarding the graduation rates of their students. Moreover, the archival information available to contemporary researchers, while invaluable, is uneven at best.

HARTFORD, CONNECTICUT
The Universal Magic of Sign Language

Homage to E. M. Gallaudet

We were disappointed to not meet at the convention Dr. Edward Miner Gallaudet, sole surviving son of Thomas Hopkins Gallaudet and founder of the national college of post-secondary education for the deaf in Washington. E. M. Gallaudet has been a champion of the combined system. We were informed that he was greatly weakened by illness and advanced age, and had been able to attend only the teachers' congress, having been driven to this by automobile. He was the object of a respectful ovation.

A motion was passed at the convention to go and present greetings at his home. Dr. Patterson was charged with organizing this visit. This was easily done and we were to meet on Woodward Avenue, in front of the famous teacher's house. President Howard took us. It was an attractive route, green with trees, with one-story houses behind plots of lawn constantly watered with a fine rain from sprinklers. We had a good half-hour's walk in the peaceful farming countryside. We almost envied the happy people who lived there in such calm and confidence.

Before one of these attractive little houses we stopped and formed up our company. Someone went forward and into the house. We saw one of the daughters of E. M. Gallaudet come out. I recognized her from her visits to Edinburgh and her father's last visit to Paris in 1900. Then one of her sisters showed up. They were both pleasantly surprised to see us. They went to get their father, who arrived supported on one arm, and was then left on his own, his body still erect although leaning on a cane. He wore a morning coat, with the cross of the French Legion of Honor spread prominently across his breast. He looked around the circle of the deaf, many of whom had been his pupils, and fingerspelled the names of those whom he recognized. Waving hands signed hurrahs and handkerchiefs were waved in salute. Tears formed behind his glasses. Then he turned toward the French delegation. He spelled out "Gaillard" in the air and I bowed. We went up the steps to shake his hand. In sign language I expressed our pleasure at seeing him again on this occasion and our hopes for his speedy recovery.

But then someone wanted to take our photograph. Chairs were brought for Gallaudet and for us. His daughters and President Howard stood behind us. This group photograph, which would consecrate the final appearance of this talented teacher in the midst of his dear intellectual heirs, was taken by Mr. MacFarlane, a member of the deaf community.

Miss Gallaudet graciously invited us to come inside. It was cozy and charming. In the master's bedroom we were shown the works of art that had been presented to him by the deaf of half a century ago. These were masterpieces of the goldsmith's craft created by deaf artists. We were also shown the wedding gown of Gallaudet's second wife, carefully preserved as a cherished relic and almost as fresh as the day it was first worn.

We came back downstairs. We found Gallaudet had taken his place in his armchair in front of his desk. The effort that he had just made, when he seemed to be in better health than at the teachers' conference, had visibly tired him. He shook our hands weakly, without a smile, his whole life concentrated in his eyes, as he nodded his head slightly. His whole attitude expressed the firmness of soul of one who knows that he is inevitably passing on, that he would see none of us again.[1] Our hearts were gripped but we showed happy faces. And if we were to weep, it would not be for him alone but for all of us, poor humans, who are brought into the world at the cost of such suffering, to a life at which we do such a poor job, and which finally ends in nothing.

Oh! To live long and well in strength, health, and goodness!

The Banquet

July 5, at eight in the evening, the grand banquet was held at the Garde Hotel. Almost 400 delegates to the convention were present. The gentlemen were in tuxedos, the ladies, numerous, attractive, and elegant, wore fashionable gowns. According to American custom, the banquet was presided over by a toastmaster. This was Michael Lapides, a most promising young man. On his right were the mayor of Hartford, the principal of the institution, Mr. Wheeler, and other notables, both hearing and deaf. On his left was the French delegation, Gaillard, Pilet, Graff, and Olivier.

The table was generously laden, but we did not see the cheery comfort of good bottles of wine. Instead, austere carafes of water and bowls in which small pieces of ice were melting. For the toasts, there was just barely a small glass filled with a finger of domestic grape juice, a kind of reddish liquid, as sharp as mulberry juice. No matter, we French, always thirsty, did justice to the ice water and signaled to the waiters to refill our glasses as often as we would have asked for more champagne at our November banquets in France.

---

1. Edward Miner Gallaudet passed away peacefully at the age of eighty-one on September 22, 1917, about three months after our visit. Profoundly religious, the conviction that he would rejoin his father among the elect supported him until his last lucid moments.

The food was nothing remarkable and the price was about three dollars. Many of the American guests thought that they could have eaten better and those who had taken part in the bicentennial celebrations for the Abbé de l'Épée in 1912 in Paris told us that for the same price they had had a much better dinner at our banquet at the Hotel Continental and had also had the pleasure of drinking our wines and champagne.

Nonetheless, we did justice to the various dishes because we had good appetites and were hungry. Just one of us was to regret it, being lightly indisposed the next day. With coffee and cigars, the toasts began. American custom has it that these should be brief and based on the topic of a maxim or quotation that was printed on the program. Thus, after the welcome toast of Frank G. Hagerty, the mayor of Hartford, Percival Hall, the president of Gallaudet College, raised a toast to education. On the program we read:

> *Utilissimo*
> Though knowledge is glorious
> Result is lasting

Frank Wheeler, the principal of the Hartford Institution, also spoke to education:

> *Elementum*
> For the best, for the noblest, for the
>   greatest
> Life and intellect

Mrs. Josephine Stewart, from Michigan, raised a toast to the Deaf Ladies of America, based on the fine lines of Shakespeare, rather enigmatic, proper to the Eternal Feminine:

> The fair, the chaste, the inexpressive She
> Speak out from thy heart that we may
>   know thee.

Thirteen toasts were listed on the program. That of the French delegation was not expected, but was added at the last moment. This relieved the superstitious of being concerned with the number thirteen. Henri Gaillard assumed responsibility for the toast and soberly limited himself to drink to the union of France and the United States in order to ensure victory over despotism, and to the solid advance of social progress, with, as corollary, the furtherance of deaf education and well-being. His toast was roundly applauded. *Gaillard was well respected*

Other toasts followed, but some of the orators, carried away by the magic of sign language, went on rather too long with their rhetoric. Even though people were complaining discreetly, the toastmaster didn't dare cut them off, but finally the moment came when he intervened. He turned toward the French delegates and signed:

Gentlemen,

I am charged by the American deaf to present to your principal delegate this symbol of esteem which we offer to the deaf of France in commemoration of the centenary celebration of the founding of the first school for the deaf in Hartford. Kindly accept it.

Mr. Michael Lapides then presented Henri Gaillard with a case containing a pure gold medal engraved with a likeness of T. H. Gallaudet on the one side, and a statement on his life's work on the other. A tiny sapphire, diamond, and ruby, the colors of France, were set in the upper part of the medal, which was strung on a tricolor ribbon. The presentation was applauded. Moved, Henri Gaillard expressed his thanks and stated that the medal would be turned over to the planned Deaf Center in Paris, where in the future the American deaf who visited the French capital would be able to find a token of the century-long friendship of their fathers for their brethren in the country of Laurent Clerc.

The banquet broke up around midnight, and the attractive ladies at the banquet adorned our tuxedo lapels with the gifts that Flora had spread over the tables.

The Mother School

I was very concerned to find a free moment to visit the school of which we were celebrating the centenary. The delay of our steamship had prevented us from arriving in time to participate in that part of the program devoted to the school. We were particularly distressed not to have seen the pageant that had been produced by Hallie Florence Gelbart, a charming and talented author who was introduced to us and to whom I expressed my deep regret at not having been able to applaud her work. A summary of other delegates' impressions follows.

The allegorical scenes were moving. The five senses were interpreted in dance by graceful girls. Suddenly, Hearting wanders off and goes looking, looking. She has lost her gift. Her companions try to console the tearful child, but then leave her. But Knowledge suddenly appears and goes toward the disconsolate child prostrate on the grass and shows her on the heights of a mountain Religion in the figure of a monk who approaches her bearing a cross. After this follow all the episodes in the education of the deaf since Aristotle and the Greeks who denied all sensation and sentiment to those who did not speak; the Christian period with St. John of Beverley; the Dutch period with Agricola (1443–1485) whom the author claims to have been the first of the learned to investigate the methodology of deaf education; the Italian one with Cardan (1501–1520), whom Miss Gelbart claims to be the first great teacher of the deaf, which is an error, since Cardan was only a theorist; the Spanish period (1520–1584) with Ponce de León and Bonet; the German period with Camerarius (1624), Schott (1642), Heinicke (1778), and Frochel (1782), who created kindergartens for pre-school learning with lessons based on everyday things and little manual tasks; the English period with Watson (1644–1800) (although Braidwood, who is not in good standing in America, was omitted); the French period with Abbé de l'Épée and Abbé Sicard from 1776; and finally the American period since 1817, the most developed as might be expected.

Here the pageant conscientiously and piously recreated the figures of Thomas Hopkins Gallaudet, Dr. Cogswell, Alice Cogswell, and Laurent Clerc.

You can imagine it: this historical kaleidoscope dominated by sign language, pantomime, and choreography must certainly have been impressive to witness. And it had a great success. The dancers were very competent and the historical actors were very numerous. The symbolic closing scene, the Future Golden Age, danced by Suzanne Gallaudet, was the final touch. There were also various school exercises and a review of the cadets of the New York Institution for the Deaf, who marched past under arms to the sound of their own military music. We shall never console ourselves for having missed what would have been an extraordinary spectacle for European eyes.

A delightful, orally trained young deaf woman, Miss Sarah Pusrin, was kind enough to serve as my guide for the visit to the institution. The institution is at the end of Asylum Avenue, not too far from the railroad station. The city is growing in this direction and in the future my force the school to relocate to a new site, where it will be less cramped and will be able to expand. There is talk of turning the area into a park. The National Association of the Deaf (NAD) would like the two monuments to Th. H. Gallaudet and Laurent Clerc, which stand on two plots of grass in front of the main building, to be incorporated in the new park. Since the pedestal of the Gallaudet monument is cracking at the base, the NAD has organized a fundraising drive to restore it.

This monument was erected in 1855 with the proceeds of campaign to which each of the American deaf contributed one cent. It generated the sum of $2,500, not a very high price at the time since the association raised about the same amount, $2,000, just to restore it. It was designed by a deaf artist, a former pupil of the Philadelphia school, Albert Newsam, but was created by hearing sculptors in Hartford, for there were no deaf sculptors at the time. The deaf painter John Carlin designed the engraving. This bas relief is the principal part of the monument and the only one of real interest. It is seated in the pedestal which holds up a pyramidal shaft topped by a sphere. The dedication to Gallaudet is on the other side of the pedestal. Although by nature a monument, the work gives a rather heavy impression. But the bas relief is very well conceived. Gallaudet is seated, wearing his teacher's coat, and is showing how the letter A is formed to a little girl whom he presses to his side while she copies the handshape. An older boy, his slate under his arm, waits for her to be initiated into the alphabet, and yet another is seated on a bench writing on his slate. All these figures are quite intelligently executed.

The monument to Laurent Clerc is the only one in the world to have been dedicated to a deaf-mute. And since it is a French deaf-mute, we have a cause for national pride. This monument, too, was erected after a fundraising campaign among the American deaf, which yielded almost $3,600. A tall, wide granite pedestal supports a bronze bust; the figure's eyes are intelligent, the face shaven with a thoughtful expression. On a bronze tablet at the base of the pedestal, his name is simply given in the letters for the manual alphabet, Clerc.

The appearance of our first American school is modest. The main building retains the look it had in 1821 when first constructed, except that covered balconies have been added at the front, and two extensions toward the rear have been added at the sides. There is nothing impressive about the entry. It gives a home-like impression, as during the time of Gallaudet and Clerc. Happily, the rooms where they liked to be have been preserved, along with the furniture, personal possessions, and books that belonged to them, including Clerc's notebooks, some dating from his time in France. There one can see that Clerc made surprisingly rapid progress in English and that Gallaudet held him in deep personal affection. There was another curious room but it was closed and no one thought of having us visit it.

Members of the National Association of the Deaf attending the centennial in Hartford

Although the ceilings are low, and the windows let in little light, the classrooms, dormitories, and dining halls are well kept. The furniture is old and worn almost everywhere but it is solid and still serviceable. The sinks are rather like those at the national institution in Paris and copper basins for washing the feet are fixed to the wooden benches. The toilet stalls, without doors, hardly seemed suitable to us, letting the pupils see each other in the acts that even kings cannot dispense with, but it seems that it is an old American custom whose purpose is to facilitate supervision.

But another building, at one side of the lawn, gave a more modern appearance. It is named Cogswell Hall. Here the stalls have doors, the sinks are clean and new, the classrooms better lit, the furniture more recently acquired and comfortable. Blackboards cover most of the available wall space. In fact, the teachers have the habit of making the pupils work side by side at the blackboards, either writing or correcting under the eye of the teacher who can then judge just how surely they master the material. As in the main building, there is a gymnasium with showers and a large hall that serves as a chapel when not used for exercises or lectures.

A bit farther off rises the little building for vocational training. On our way there, we met the deaf typography teacher,
Walter Durian. Very kindly, he showed us the way to a shop
sufficiently spacious for the number of pupils that he instructs.
There is a printing press on which they print the house newspaper *The New Era*, and we were given an issue. Among the
assignments carried out by pupils to help determine their grades
for the year we noted an article about Marshal Joffre by young
Clarence Baldwin. It was a biography and its accuracy was surprising from an adolescent and would have surprised the marshal if he had learned that it was the work of a young speaking
deaf man. He wrote that Joffre was "a man on the model of
Lincoln and Grant, made reasonable by responsibility, and
haunted by the misfortunes of his nation." The paper also had
a section reserved for the activities of alumni.

The institution formerly bore the name of "Asylum for
Deaf-Mutes." This explains why the avenue that leads to the
school still carries that name. At the convention, it was proposed that the municipality be approached with a view to having this absurd name changed and replaced by the more
justified and glorious one of "Avenue Gallaudet." As the local
bylaw requires, the motion was submitted to the owners and
tenants of houses along the avenue. A majority of votes showed
that the residents had no intention of changing this part of their
address. Thus, even in the United States, popular custom can
dominate the concern for posthumous homage to the benefactors of the city.

But the board of trustees of the institution, especially after
a campaign waged by the deaf, had earlier agreed to alter the
name of the school. The present name is "The American
School at Hartford for the Deaf." This name is also more dig-
nified, beautiful, and justified. The school opened on April 15,
1817, with seven pupils and two teachers—two geniuses, the
hearing American of French extraction, Thomas Hopkins Gallaudet, and the deaf Frenchman, Laurent Clerc. From this
mother school, popularly conceived of as an asylum, sprang

157 schools with 14,309 pupils, 1,944 teachers, and one post-secondary college. Name one European country that can claim to have done as much.

Mr. Frank R. Wheeler is the principal of the institution. We had only caught a glimpse of him during a brief presentation at the convention. But he appeared an intelligent and skillful teacher, an accomplished signer. Everywhere we went, people praised him, stressing his commitment and his will to further advances in the school's instruction. He is assisted by twenty teachers, nine vocational instructors, and eleven supervisors of both sexes. There were 232 pupils enrolled in the 1915–1916 school year, 117 boys and 115 girls. Costs for almost all of them are borne by their home states, for they do not all come from Connecticut, but also from Massachusetts, New Hampshire, Vermont, and even Maine and Rhode Island. Pupils are admitted from the age of four. There are even occasional pupils between sixteen and twenty. Twenty-seven percent of the pupils are congenitally deaf; 6 percent with discovery or onset within the first year of life; 7 percent between the ages of two and three; 1 percent each at the ages of four, six, eight, and twelve years; and 10 percent undocumented.

Oral instruction is given to the majority of pupils, especially those newly admitted, who are transferred to the manual classes only when their progress is unsatisfactory. There are sixteen oral classes as opposed to three manual classes taught by deaf teachers. In the first year, the teaching is slowly paced so that pupils get a sense of speech rhythms and tone.

The annual budget of the school amounts to $74,620, of which $58,000 comes from the states. The law in Connecticut provides for every deaf minor who has not passed the age of twelve to be admitted.

Silent Sports

As we were again crossing the grounds, we saw, off in the distance, a crowd of deaf men and women standing or seated on benches that bordered a large open area. These young people, in white shorts and colored jerseys bearing large cabalistic letters on the chest, with bare arms and legs, and bright, young, perspiring faces, were placed as if on a chessboard. Miss Sarah Pusrin informed me that it was a game of baseball. This is the American national sport. On the transatlantic steamer on our way to America, one of my cordial co-passengers, Mr. Beckwith, a prominent American veterinarian who was returning from having overseen a shipment of horses to Saint-Nazaire, had explained this rather complicated sport to me. I tried to follow the game. But for many of those there, I was an even greater curiosity. I especially had to answer the questions of some charming but none too tactful young women. Still, I could understand that the two silent opposing teams were equally matched, equally skillful, and astonishingly quick. Yet the game seemed heated and brutal to me. The goalkeeper wore a metal mask over his face, proof of how dangerous it was to be struck by the ball.

Several deaf baseball teams had come to Hartford. The rivalry among the clubs is quite serious, but affects only this national specialty, which was then at the midpoint in its season.

I didn't see any cyclists, but there must certainly have been great numbers of them. Springtime would have been a better season for organizing bicycle races. If one of our French deaf champions had wanted to make the voyage to test himself against an American racer, he would clearly have had a real match.

Football, the American variety, is also a very popular sport here. It is even taught in the schools. At almost all the institutions for the deaf there are teams of young football players who, when they leave school, can simply join teams of adult deaf players. Among the latter, some teams become so strong that they can beat even well-known hearing teams. But this sport is so violent that there are often accidents, even fatal ones on occasion. A young woman told me that she was inconsolable after the death of her fiancé who had been killed by a blow to the head during an overly rough scrimmage. Let this be a warning to the impetuous.

Basketball is another competitor sport. And there are bowling and billiards, as well as all kinds of other games. The deaf newspapers often publish accounts of deaf athletes and players who have beaten their hearing counterparts, even at chess.

Whether it is competitive sport, recreational sport, fitness activities such as swimming, or games of skill, the American deaf reach a very high level of competence. Their coaches have quite rightly not thought that the fact of being deprived of the sense of hearing precluded the right to become healthy and strong, alert, attractive, and graceful. This is why physical education in the form of gymnastics and outdoor sports is promoted just as actively as religious, moral, and intellectual training. Thus the Americans succeed in making their students almost fully realized human beings. In France, we can also find some schools that have this integral conception of education, naturally also encompassing deaf students, but progress is slow. The example of deaf athletic clubs encourages us to follow this course. However, many of our schools should not be faulted. They lack the appropriate resources. It is up to the various levels of government to provide the necessary subsidies.

[handwritten margin note: so b/c lack of one sense, awareness increases?]

[handwritten note: Football huddles began by deaf players (its signed on field, opposing team would read more)]

Driving

There is a particular form of sport that is beginning to be popular, at least among the well-off deaf. But this is something quite unexpected, which runs headlong into prejudice, particularly from legislators and administrators, who turn their erroneous judgments into absurd laws and ridiculous prohibitions. This is quite simply the case with automobilism.

There are some American states that forbid the deaf to drive automobiles and others that see no problem in issuing licenses after a serious examination. This is more or less what happens in

France, where we find one chief of police opposed to a deaf businessman calling on customers in his jurisdiction and others, even the chief of police of Paris, who license such drivers after congratulating them on passing the examination.

The pretext of those opposed is that a deaf driver may cause accidents in oncoming traffic and especially that he risks being struck from behind by cars that he does not hear coming.

By this reasoning, it should be forbidden to all deaf and hard of hearing to walk around as pedestrians on the streets and roads.

In fact, for driving an automobile or even a horse and carriage hearing is of no use. Vision alone is important. And ability and a cool head. With the noise of the wheels, even those with rubber tires, the vibrations of the motors, the clamor of the busy streets, one's hearing is overwhelmed. But the driver who looks attentively ahead as well as in all other directions, who steers the vehicle skillfully, avoids obstacles, and has a concern for human life, he has no need to hear. Full attention is assured by his eye and mind. He will not be concerned with the juvenile fear that those behind him will run into him. He trusts their ability. He knows that he is protected by police regulations and traffic laws. And, in the unlikely event that he were struck from behind, it would only be the result of some chance occurrence that no sharpness of hearing would have been able to prevent: skidding, swerving, some mechanical aberration of the vehicle, or the sudden insanity of a driver who lost all sense of direction. Clearly, such cases are rare. One chance in a hundred. It is not for such petty reasons that we should shudder at the idea of confiding to the deaf these torpedoes reaching speeds of sixty miles an hour. Even more than among the hearing, their attentiveness is multiplied hundredfold in the exteriorization of their inner concentration.

In actual fact, scarcely any accidents are reported as due to deaf drivers. The only one that has occurred can be attributed not to deafness but to impulsiveness and carelessness, one of those lapses from prudence that even the hearing are prone to

[margin annotation: Wouldn't music distract the hearing?]

in the company of infatuated and playful young women. Two young men and two girls got into an automobile that belonged to one of them, and were laughing, having fun, gesturing, and busy giving each other long and intoxicating kisses. The driver, hanging from the lips of his girlfriend, did he not see that he was about to cross railway tracks? Or did he think he could make it across in time? An express train came rushing down, and sent the lightly built vehicle tumbling down the track ahead of it, and sent two or three of its occupants to the Kingdom of Death. Cupid plays cruel tricks, even with our peaceful and comfortable modern inventions! A confidential word of advice to young people, whether hearing or not: on the road, watch the road and you are more certain of looking into the eyes of your blonde or brunette at a time when you can relax with that pleasant pastime, that is, at the end of your excursion.

In one state where the governor had forbidden the deaf to drive automobiles, one of them wrote offering to drive him safely wherever he wanted to go. The governor initially turned him a deaf ear, perhaps too afraid of having his ribs broken in the company of such an eccentric with obstructed hearing. But the deaf man was so persistent and insistent that the governor finally gave in.

Moreover, in the automobiles of all the deaf persons who were kind enough to drive us around, we noted that they had mounted on the front of the vehicle a mirror that reflected everything that was happening on the road behind. Thus, if they saw that they were being closely followed, when they wanted to make a turn or pass other automobiles, they extended their hand as a signal to slow up a bit, and they then made their maneuver without mishap.

At the Moving Pictures

That evening, an automobile driven by the deaf Mr. Faucher came at the request of President Howard to fetch us and bring us to the institute where the auditorium had been arranged for a program of moving pictures.

This was the first time that we had been in an automobile driven by one of the silent. I was quite prepared for the way in which he would give us a sample of the art of breaking people's ribs with clumsy swerves. Or this at least is the public and administrative prejudice in certain localities which, in other respects, are not off in Never Never Land.

It was dusk. There were blinding lights and shadowy corners, automobiles and pedestrians. Suddenly, with a light and quick movement as if in a game, Mr. Faucher turned smoothly to the side and in a few rapid minutes had dropped us off safe and sound at the door of the institution.

To think that there are people who would not confide their precious person to a deaf driver! Evidently, it is an environment even more dangerous than that of a submarine or bomber.

The program had already begun. And these were not ordinary, poorly edited, everyday moving pictures. It was cinema for the deaf by the deaf—the re-creation of deaf settings, the events of deaf social life, the delivery of speeches signed by well-known deaf people and by beloved teachers whose features are thus assured of being handed down to posterity along with their winged words, their ideas, and their counsel. There was a whole series of films that are part of the patrimony of the National Association of the Deaf. A special Moving Pictures Fund had been set up, with its own resources. The films are screened at national conventions. They can also be loaned to local societies and to schools for the instruction of students.

We in France should be inspired by this example and, to begin with, ought to try to obtain the films that were shot on the occasion of the bicentenary of the Abbé de l'Épée at Versailles in 1912, so that they might be preserved and cherished. This would transmit to the future the eloquent countenance and gestures of the great orator of the deaf, Ernest Dusuzeau.

The auditorium was filled and it was oppressively warm. Many men took off their jackets and I did the same.

On the screen was a rendition of *The Song of Hiawatha*, the famous poem by the great American poet Longfellow. A deaf woman was performing. She was slim and attractive, with harmonious gestures, slow and clear, in a rhythm like that of the verses, with flowing movements that came and went from one end to the other of the wooded landscape through which she passed.

I have read Longfellow's poem in English, ravishing and moving, from beginning to end. But, because I came in during the performance, I did not know exactly where the performer was in the poem. With a succession of gestures, which were not the simple pantomime we practice in France in order to be understood by a wider public, but were conventional signs, she frequently fingerspelled the names of Hiawatha and Minnehaha:

> Brought the sunshine of his people
> Minnehaha, Laughing Water,
> Handsomest of all the women,
> In the land of the Dakotas,
> In the land of handsome women.

With inspired fervor and a perfect sense of the poetry, the graceful interpreter completed her performance, showing in sovereign fashion that sign language with its infinite shadings can express the most subtle ideas in the verses of any language.

Then there passed across the screen a sequence of speeches signed by hearing and deaf teachers: Hotchkiss, Schuyler Long (who spoke against the abuse of imaginative admixtures to sign language and promoted signing in the classical style), Fay, and Edward Miner Gallaudet. There was something strangely impressive to see him on the screen, signing as he did several years ago at a convention of the deaf, this beloved teacher who was soon to enter the kingdom of shadows, the fatal land of *Nevermore*, to which we all inexorably advance. But at least through the marvelous invention of cinema and the brilliant idea of the National

Association of the Deaf to establish its archive of silent films, his image and those of his prominent students and disciples will live for the eyes of the future in gratitude and honor. Oh! If only there had been moving pictures at the time of the Abbé de l'Épée!

Another interesting feature of the program was the screening of episodes from life at Gallaudet College: graduation day, students and professors filing past in gowns, mortarboards on their heads; students acting in a play depicting Thomas Hopkins Gallaudet giving lessons to Alice Cogswell, his first pupil. The costumes, the exact decor of the period, the resemblance to the actual persons, everything was as it should be!

But the program went on, and in the building next door was a dance, which we had promised to attend. We slipped out.

The Dance

Dancing is among the most popular pastimes in the United States. The deaf couldn't imagine being left out! Their associations, especially in winter, frequently organize large dances that are also happily attended by the hearing. And the members, despite their deafness, are excellent dancers. The deaf ladies are notable for their passion for the waltz. Even if they do not hear the music, many of them sense the vibrations. In any case, they have rhythm in their legs and those who are well practiced in the steps and turns have no need of the musical accompaniment. The choreographed movements follow one another effortlessly, in the kicks, the studied whirls, spins, and jumps. And if they dance with hearing partners, they have no need to look at the floor to get the steps right.

Here in Hartford, they had reserved the gymnasium for the dance. There were quite a few people present, although fewer than I had seen in Chicago in 1893. And they were all young. The pretty misses, with stylish hair and necklines and bright summer dresses, spread their gaiety and exuberance. They quickly surrounded the French delegates. Miss Sarah Pusrin and her sister were among the friendliest. They absolutely insisted on having us dance. But, alas! None of us knew how. We should have brought along other Parisian followers of Terpsichore. We had to satisfy ourselves with flirting, which is also a very Parisian art, one that is very agreeable to students of human nature, as we were.

At Lake Compounce

Saturday had been reserved for the traditional countryside excursion that concludes all the larger get-togethers of the deaf. The morning was radiant, the afternoon superb, the evening delicious.

The organizing committee had chartered several streetcars. Parked opposite the institution, they were stormed by hundreds of the deaf, while others preferred to stay behind.

It proved a very long ride along tracks lined with trees, across endless fields, then passing through unexpected towns and industrial areas.

Finally, under the cover of a little woods, we came upon the lake, a natural lake at the foot of some low hills, and hardly larger than Lake Enghien in Belgium. It is a recreational area for the residents of Hartford and surroundings. All around were pavilions with restaurants, bars, soda fountains, stands selling candy and souvenirs, games and contests of various kinds, a roller-coaster and rides, shooting galleries. On the lakeshore, many canoes for rent and huts for swimmers to change.

Once we arrived, Mr. Pach took a large posed photograph that gathered the greatest possible number of participants. Then we proceeded to lunch in a huge restaurant. Light dishes, or beef and boiled potatoes were the main course, accompanied by coffee.

After that, people went off to follow their own preferences and fancy. Lovers went off to lose themselves in the undergrowth of the woods. Others headed for the games and rides. Some went canoeing. One deaf gentleman, Mr. Walter Glover from South Carolina, treated us to a ride in two rowboats. Two of the French delegation were good rowers, Monsieur Graf and Monsieur Olivier, and their colleagues, seated opposite them, Monsieur Gaillard and Monsieur Pilet, had only to let themselves be lulled for two hours by the gentle waves in the company of charming misses. It was delightful to drift along with the babbling water thinking that long ago beautiful Indian maidens had paddled here in their dugout canoes.

Mr. Walter Glover and several others insisted on taking our pictures with small snapshot cameras. Even Mr. Glover himself, who was very tall, wanted his picture taken with Monsieur Henri Gaillard, the pygmy of the French delegation, so that we could make an amusing comparison with two eccentric American comics who had the music halls in stitches, Mutt and Jeff.

I speak of Mr. Walter Glover in the past tense. Unfortunately, this fine young man is no longer with us, having died rather suddenly three or four months ago. He was an enthusiastic friend of France and dreamed of coming on a visit after the war to Paris with his sister, who is also deaf. In his hometown, he was very attached to a deaf woman, of distant French Huguenot descent, Miss Theresa E. Gaillard, a former student of Gallaudet College, who by a curious coincidence bore the same family name as the leader of the French delegation.

The hours passed slowly and gently. Then, members of the hearing community began to appear. The American Saturday afternoon frees up all its city workers who rush to all possible kinds of entertainment. We saw a large group of girls sporting red, white, and blue ribbons on their stylish straw hats of various kinds. Were they French or was it a sign of patriotic support? There was not even a moment to permit the indiscretion of asking them. The agile nymphs had quickly disappeared behind the rocks.

A luxury automobile passed, filled with deaf persons who could spend their dollars without keeping track. Smiling greetings were exchanged and then the well-heeled group was already gone.

Suddenly, there was a rush to the lakeshore. A young deaf swimmer had gone down, and now a courageous rescuer, a deaf Canadian named M. W. Rourke, brought him back to the beach. This was not his first save and we all congratulated him warmly.

Then came the superb sunset in an apotheosis of blue and gold. We resumed our seats in the streetcars. Our good luck put us in the company of some pretty young deaf women whom we had not met earlier. They were so witty, like all Americans, that the ride seemed a short one, even though it was a two-hour trip back to Hartford.

Here we express our cordial thanks to the organizers of the centennial celebration: Mr. J. E. Crane, president, Miss Mary E. Atkinson, secretary, J. O. Moran, treasurer, and W. C. Rockwell, H. T. Faucher, G. L. Bonham, F. J. Bonvouloir, Michel Lapides, etc. They gave the French delegates a reception that will always be remembered.

The Frat

Saturday, July 7, after our return from Lake Compounce, at eight o'clock in the evening, we went to the meeting of those members of the National Fraternal Society of the Deaf who had attended the Hartford celebration.

I had known for quite some time about the existence of this society, founded more or less on the model of the Société d'Appui fraternel des Sourds-Muets de France (Society for the Fraternal Support of the Deaf of France) that had been established in Paris by Monsieur Joseph Cochefer in 1879. I knew about its rapid, enthusiastic expansion and its objectives of strict solidarity. At the convention I had met many members who bore its insignia: a circle with a star, surrounded by chains that ended in two clasped hands, the symbol of fraternal attachment. After learning that the society had planned a meeting on the fringe of the convention, I expressed my desire to attend with my co-delegates and spoke to some members, in particular Mr. Alexander and Mr. Shea, the latter being the organizer for New York State. They promised to arrange for our attendance.

As a matter of fact, attendance was not easy for people who were not members, and the entrances were guarded by grim doorkeepers who had been given the assignment of enforcing strict security. This we experienced when the guards, oblivious of our status as Frenchmen, stated politely but firmly that we could not enter, especially during the debates that were taking place. They said they would inform the society's board and showed us to a waiting room where we found a dozen deaf young men, who all appeared anxious and replied distractedly to our questions. It was only later that we understood the reasons for this strange behavior. These were candidates for membership who were now going to be definitively admitted to the society after a month's probation. But first they had to submit to the initiation tests and ritual. They racked their brains over the unknown ordeal that they would have to undergo, just like members of a catechism class at the moment when they are to plunge into the dark of the confessional.

The waiting period grew longer and, like Monsieur Filet, I began to become impatient and spoke of leaving, when Mr. Alexander, or rather Brother Alexander, showed up. The rule of the society was that all members were brothers and were so called. Mr. Alexander entered the sanctuary and then came back to say that the board requested that we have a little more patience. No debate could be interrupted. He also admonished us not to reveal, at least in America, what we were about to witness. We kept our promise on that count. But in writing these pages, we judge ourselves freed of our pledge. And as both a sociologist and a moralist, I have an interest in making the truth known.

Finally, we were admitted. We bowed on entering, while the president rose and designated seats for us on his left. What a strange chamber! Completely closed off and sealed. All the windows were shut and draped. On the walls were the banners of the society's branches that were represented, inscriptions with texts on solidarity and fraternity, appeals to attend the great convention in Los Angeles in 1921. The members of the board were seated on a small and very narrow stage at the far end of the room. The president had only a small table before him. At his two sides, below and at some distance, were tables for the secretary and treasurer, and, on chairs around the walls, the members grouped by branch association, from time to time with an officer seated in front at a table covered with a mat arranged in a special manner. All the space in the center of the room had been left empty. Alone in the middle was a cabalistic pedestal table, topped by a mysterious box which was in turn covered by a cloth like a stole. Evidently, the Frat constituted a kind of deaf Freemasonry. The bylaws, in fact, state that the society is instituted on the model of a lodge with ritual procedures and a representative form of government.

The president, Mr. Laurence W. Crowley, rose and greeted us. He welcomed us to the Frat and I thanked him. I said that having passionately read all the deaf American newspapers that I exchanged for our paper, I had been able to follow the development of the society since its inception and that I wholeheartedly applauded its activities. I congratulated its founders and its officers, and I praised the solidarity and fraternity that bore up the individual and gave him consciousness of his personal value, rather than the charity that pulls down and depresses, and is acceptable only in the face of a threat of undeserved misfortune. Monsieur Pilet, in turn, expressed his surprise at finding such a powerful organization that exercised mutuality on such a vast scale. Monsieur Jean Olivier also expressed his pleasure at being present and drew a comparison with the local French society in Champagne that had a capital fund of almost 200,000 francs despite the invasion of the barbarous Germans. Monsieur Graff explained that he earlier worked toward the success of a society founded on almost the same principles, the Society for the Fraternal Support of the Deaf of France. Unfortunately, the vanity of its founding president in discouraging the devoted efforts of his most zealous collaborators had negatively affected the for-

tunes of the organization. He trusted that its American counterpart would not suffer a similar fate, since it was not founded
on the exercise of personal power and because each of its members submitted to social discipline and to reason.

The French delegation was roundly applauded.

The session resumed. Reports were made of social activities
and a discussion followed. A member who wished to speak would
rise, extend his hand while bowing, like the greeting of the
ancient Romans. A member who wished to leave excused himself in the same fashion, as did a member who entered. Thus,
order ruled and nothing escaped the president's eye.

But then the lights were being lowered. Darkness suddenly
reigned except around some lamps turned down to the level of
nightlights. And from the other end of the chamber there entered
in single file a train of persons in black gowns and hoods, followed by our dozen novices in their ordinary clothes, their eyes
blindfolded and their trousers drawn up to expose one bare leg.

The initiation rites were to begin.

The novices waited in a row. One at a time they came forward to the hooded figures. Each one had his inquisitor. These
pretended to stab their leg, making deep cuts and causing blood
to flow, all by special effects that gave the desired impression. If
the initiate did not tremble, did not cry out, it was proof that
he had the strength of character to make him a faithful and convinced member of the society. The tests varied in kind. The
novices were made to respond by signing with their eyes still covered. An exception was made for a former student of the oral
method who did not understand sign language and whose blind-
fold was lifted so that he could lipread. Then, the initiates were
conducted to the lighted area. There, one of the interrogators
repeated for each of the candidates a signed formula requiring
them to swear to submit to the rules of the society and to practice absolute fraternity with their colleagues. Each one took the
oath. When this had been accomplished, the interrogator
announced to the president that these probationary candidates
were desirable future members of the society. Then their blind-

folds were removed. The president asked them further questions and declared them admitted to the society.

Brother Pach directed the admission tests. But the initiation was not yet over. The candidates were obliged to stand for all kinds of burlesque hazing: crawling into a barrel that was then rolled across the floor, picking things up with their mouth, etc. Perhaps this amused the spectators, but we found it a bit tiresome, and even pointless. We had a better appreciation of the first part of the initiation, which sought to test the will and sincerity of the new members.

In France, things are simpler. The candidate for membership must be proposed by two sponsors and if, at the end of a month, there is no opposition and the membership fee has been paid, the applicant is accepted. But it is true that many do not display the spirit of fidelity and fraternity that inspires the American deaf.

After these ceremonies, delicious refreshments and sandwiches were served. The Hartford Frat does things on a generous scale.

A canvas by Brother Alexander, representing Thomas Hopkins Gallaudet, was unveiled; it had been purchased by the Hartford branch to decorate its meeting room. The portrait was well painted, in the strong, expressive manner that characterized the talent of Jack Alexander.

On parting, we thanked the board of the Hartford Thirty-Seventh Division, Messrs. Crowley, Bonvouloir, Moran, Luther, Mottram, Hale, Dermody, Smith, Robert Saint-Jean, Blanchard, Cossette, Frazier, Barrows, Olson, Fricke, and also the delegate from the Eastern Division based in Chicago, the Reverend Flick.

Now, let's explain just what the National Fraternal Society of the Deaf really is.

As documentation, we have its constitution and bylaws, and its official organ, *The Frat*, a monthly publication of sixteen three-column pages, subscription to which is compulsory for all members of the society.

The Frat is concerned primarily with the society itself but does not neglect questions that further the interests of the deaf. It provides news of the branches, reviews the financial position of the society, gives the background of new members, marriage announcements, deaths, and births from among the membership, board decisions, a list of honor of *Sons with the Colors*, the hearing children of the deaf serving in the Armed Forces, plus articles on the mutual insurance scheme, the economy, pensions, etc. As you can see, it is intelligently conceived and it has an excellent editor in Mr. Francis P. Gibson, the principal secretary, in Chicago.

At the beginning of the constitution is found this tutelary rule: "The members of this Society, recognizing the existence of a Supreme Being who controls earthly affairs and before whose justice and mercy we incline ourselves, vow to conduct the affairs of our Society in accord with this belief."

The aim of the society is to reunite fraternally all qualified white deaf men between the ages of eighteen and fifty-five (the age limit for admission) who are of sound constitution and mental health, and are of good character and diligent industry; to grant them moral aid and succor in the case of necessity; to establish a fund to assist sick or temporarily incapacitated members; to pay varying sums of money on the death of a member to persons whom the deceased has designated in accord with the bylaws. The society also seeks to advance honor, fraternity, public-spiritedness in its members; to encourage industry, ambition, honesty, and perseverance; to avoid, if possible, that they be blamed, cheated, or imposed on, that they be maltreated in any fashion that would appear malicious or disgraceful.

The society is divided into a Grand Division and subordinate sections. The Grand Division includes the Grand Officers who are the principal administrators and delegates from each of the sections. The sections comprise members from localities, towns, and cities who have received the right of self-government from the board of trustees of the Grand Division. Frat members then belong to a local society that is under the supervision and direction of the Grand Division and its officers. A convention of all the members or of their delegates is held every three years in July in a locality determined at the previous convention. The board of directors may decide to hold special conventions. It would be difficult to analyze completely here the statutes that amount to sixty pages of text, in two parts: the constitution with twenty-four articles and the bylaws with twenty-three, some of which run to twelve paragraphs. There is an index at the back of the booklet which permits members to orient themselves. Like most American legislation, it is dense and detailed.

The duties of the grand president are given on one page, those of the grand secretary on two, the treasurer on three. You can then judge the importance of the matters that they have to deal with. The officers of the Grand Division are paid, that is, they either receive a fixed salary or are paid for specific duties performed. It is an absolute principle in America, among the hearing as well as the deaf, that all those who devote their talent, time, and effort to the public or a collective interest should be paid more or less according to what is needed for them to consecrate themselves entirely to such work or to commit a substantial amount of their free time. In this fashion, the officers are more conscientious and zealous, which explains the prosperity of their undertakings and the general progress of the deaf cause.

In France, credit must be given to the Société d'appui fraternel (Society for Fraternal Support) of Monsieur Cochefer, which is nearly the only one to have applied this moral and democratic principle of paying for services rendered. The secretary and treasurer are exempted from paying the membership fee and are reimbursed for expenses incurred on behalf of the society. It is little enough, I am sure, but it is important to realize that by remunerating hard-working officers you get real results. The Frat even awards commissions to those who sign up members for insurance to offset funeral costs.

Not all the deaf are admitted to the fraternity. Those who work in bars, beer parlors, distilleries, and those who overindulge in alcohol are excluded. The same applies to those who work with chemical products and toxic substances, such as painters and varnishers, miners, railroad employees, high tension electricians, steelworkers, and generally all those who are engaged in work that carries the risk of sudden or rapid death.

Life insurance benefits are not paid to the heirs of those who die as the result of accidents while walking along railways or highways, alcoholism (delirium tremens, cirrhosis of the liver), football, baseball (except in the case of professionals), basketball, boxing, bicycle, motorcycle or automobile racing, altercations, dissolute living, and suicide.

Life insurance policies are available for sums of $250, $500, $1,000, $1,500, and even $2,000. For coverage in the $250 range, a twenty-one year old would pay 24 cents a month; a thirty-year old, 31 cents; at age forty, the policy payment is 44 cents; at fifty, 68 cents, at fifty-five, 86 cents. The equivalent charge for a $1,000 policy is $0.93, $1.22, $1.76, $2.71, and $3.44, respectively. In addition, the monthly membership cost is 35 cents; this includes health and accident insurance, as well as covering the association's general costs. The sign-up fee is $5.

The financial report for 1917 shows that the organization received $46,900 in membership fees. It spent $4,000 on funeral expenses, awarded $4,715 for accidents and illnesses, about $3,000 for the officers' salaries, and just over $1,000 for the publication of the house organ *The Frat*. With a combined capital and income of $168,247, and expenses of $15,884, the society ended its fiscal year with a capital of $152,363. What a wonderful accomplishment!

Each month, *The Frat* publishes at the head of its editorial page the laconic but eloquent figure of the society's assets as of the last day of the previous month. In the February issue we find $157,170.70. The society advances, ever more vigorous: 3,137 members, sixty-three sections, number one of which is in Chicago, with number sixty-three in Dallas, Texas. In reality, the first section should be, historically, that of Detroit, for it was a group of former pupils from the Flint Institution who, fifteen years ago, conceived the idea of a deaf lodge, based on secret rituals, discretion, and mutual assistance, like those operated by the hearing. But because it was necessary to locate the administrative seat of the organization in a large city, Chicago was chosen. It is from this gigantic city that a handful of intelligent deaf people in a spirit of social solidarity administer the silent American fraternity and produce its multiple benefits. Here are their names and offices:

Grand Division

Grand President: Harry C. Anderson, Indianapolis, bank employee

First Vice President: William L. Davis, Philadelphia, railroad administrator

Second Vice President: H. Lorraine Tracy, Baton Rouge, minister of the Episcopalian Church

Third Vice President: Arthur L. Roberts, Olathe, Kansas, teacher at the Kansas Institution

Grand Secretary: François P. Gibson, Chicago. A full-time employee who is paid $166.66 monthly

Deputy Secretary: Edward M. Rowse, Chicago. Similarly full-time, paid $83.33/month

Treasurer: Washington Barrow, insurance company clerk

Trustees:

George F. Flick, President, Chicago, minister of the Deaf Episcopalian church of Chicago

Horace W. Buell, Chicago, business employee

Harrison M. Leiter, Chicago, bank employee

We could have wished that a similar agency, so useful and so powerful, had succeeded in France. However, it would not be difficult to get it back on its feet.

At the Cemeteries

On behalf of the French deaf we had brought two bronze palm fronds to be placed on the tombs of T. H. Gallaudet and Laurent Clerc. But this was not a simple matter, since American cemeteries are run in a different way from those in France. We then agreed that we would leave our palms with the institution, which would have them mounted at the base of the Gallaudet and Clerc monuments, or would preserve them in its museum. Beforehand, and this was in particular the idea of the reception committee and of Felix Bonvouloir, it was arranged that we would briefly place the palms on the earth that covered the remains of the two founders and that we would then bring them back. In addition, we wanted to see the graves. The difficulty was that the new cemetery where Gallaudet rested was very far from the city. But Mr. Rockwell, a speaking deaf automobile owner, the son of a rich industrialist in Hartford and a former student at Gallaudet College, offered us his car. Sunday morning we climbed in, Graff, Pilet, and I, in the company of Mr. Parsons who was to be our guide.

Mr. Rockwell was a marvelous driver. His automobile rolled along deftly and rapidly, actually adding a bit of freshness to the close morning air. The course that we took was of several miles.

The cemetery, mostly reserved for the affluent, was like a park and gave a imposing monumental impression. Trees, huge shrubs, wide drives, a stream with weeping willows along its banks, vast lawns from which rose, each at some distance from the other, the monuments erected in memory of the dead. Most of these were huge funerary urns, some quite lavish, other with real artistic merit, but very few crosses. There was nothing stuffy, closed in, tangled up, loaded with the mortuary bric-à-brac that you see in Parisian cemeteries. No, here everything was severe and simple, well spaced and clean, and on the whole so majestic that one did not at all have the feeling of sadness that you might have before a simple grave behind a country church.

Then we stood before the graves of the Gallaudets. In the middle of them was the tombstone of Thomas Hopkins Gallaudet, which carried a brief inscription. All around it, in a concentric circle, were spaced small gravestones set in the grass, giving the names of his children, grandchildren, the first wife of Edward Miner, his second wife and, a bit in front, a low cross indicating the final resting place of a clergyman, the Rev. Thomas Gallaudet, the founder of the American church of the deaf. Next to him was the plaque of his wife, a good and well known deaf woman. The whole family is now reunited there.

We deposed our bronze palm on the grass and we bowed our uncovered heads.

Now the automobile was taking us to Clerc's cemetery. An older one, it was located in a distant part of the city, in front of houses that were still occupied and closed off with only an iron gate. The graves were close together as in Europe and were not even situated in a regular pattern. This was the old-fashioned system. In order to locate the tomb of our fellow countryman we had to walk over the grounds. It was marked by a vertical plaque shaped like a pointed church window; it looked old and weathered, but the inscription was still visible. The words *born at La Balme (France)* moved us. On the sides were the graves of his wife and of a son. We placed our palm on the ground and I picked some leaves from a shrub growing behind the tombstone of Laurent Clerc.

Mr. Rockwell drove us back to the hotel to get our luggage and drive it to the station, for we were to leave Hartford in the afternoon. Then his automobile dropped us off in front of the institution. We had been invited to lunch by the cordial and devoted matron, Miss Atkinson, who stood in for the absent principal. Some of the senior teachers, among whom were two or three deaf ones, joined us. It was a pleasant and tasty luncheon, and was accompanied by charming conversation. We thanked Miss Atkinson for having put such a telling final touch to the impression that we had gained of Hartford, the Mecca of American teaching of the deaf.

President Howard

He is a man of great distinction, of high intellectual and moral stature, and especially of dynamic energy. Much better than a skillful but impartial president, he devoted three years of his life to the prosperity of the powerful national association and to the progress of the deaf in both school and society. He is a fully accomplished businessman. Within this category, to which a number of the American deaf have won access, he occupies a perhaps unique rank. He is a banker, in fact, a private banker. He succeeded his father as the head of a financial company, and has barely two or three management employees. But he is in charge. He is the head of the Howard Investment Company and its earnings rise from year to year. All the capital that is entrusted to his care increases, either through the purchase of property and houses or through mortgages. However, my ignorance of American financial operations, whose mechanisms appear much more complicated than those in France and which are free to operate under the overall control of the state, does not permit me to give a better appreciation of the nature of Mr. Howard's affairs. All that I can say according to the documents that I have is that just as securely as in an insurance company and even more rapidly, he makes the savings that are confided to him prosper.

If we had been able to accept his kind invitation to go to the northern city of Duluth, it would have been simple to inspect his company and to get a better idea of his managerial skills. The spectacle of a deaf man handling the money of others with skill, integrity, and a rare power of will would be of great interest for sociologists and friends of the deaf. And it is a fine example for the deaf that he is favored by good fortune as well as by intelligence.

The Garde Hotel

This is the headquarters of the deaf. Many stay there but all the deaf gather in the huge, high-ceilinged foyer on the ground floor.

It gives a rather curious effect, this crowd of silent people standing and gesturing, while others sit in rocking chairs or relax in huge armchairs, reading giant newspapers fresh off the presses, which consecrate wide columns to the activities of the convention. One of them even had this headline in large type: *Dr. Gaillard will speak for France in sign language.* Taking me for a doctor is really too much.

But I can't deny that we were an attraction and we enjoyed chatting with one and all. Several invited us to have some fresh beer, or an iced ginger ale in the adjacent bar or in the salon where ladies were permitted. As they say in English, we really had "a good time."

From the street and through the bay windows that had been opened, you could see this pandemonium of intermingled and multiplied signs. Passers-by looked at us without making fun or fuss and went on their way. Even the newspaper boys stayed respectful. We ran into a charming little girl who spoke to us with the manual alphabet. It would seem that in America public education about the deaf is more successful than in France.

Another new sight for us were the meetings between deaf persons every few steps as they came and went. They would greet each other and continue on their way, unless they were close friends. This rare vision of a street where all the residents were deaf would be revealed to us again in Akron. In France, we already have a glimpse of such a community in Billancourt-Boulogne where numerous deaf people work in the local aircraft factories. Ah! The universal magic of sign language!

NEW YORK, THE FIRST VISIT
To Every Man His Due

The express train from Hartford to New York took about four
hours. Along with us were Mr. Spear and Mr. Pach, two remarkable deaf businessmen. Mr. Spear is a manufacturer of envelopes
in Minneapolis.[1] He invented a system of envelopes for samples
with an ingenious closing device that prevents material from
being lost but since it was not sealed could be mailed for less
cost. He was the official supplier to the Department of Agriculture, which gave him large orders for envelopes for shipping seed
grain. Before that, he had been the founder and principal of the
North Dakota school, but had resigned following some local dis-
agreements. To him goes the credit of establishing the labor
office for the deaf in the state of Minnesota. He almost looks
French, with a pointed beard like King Henri III. His face is so
different from the American faces around us that some people
take him for one of the French delegates. Actually, he is Cana-

---

1. Since our return to France we learned of the death of Mr. Spear, who
was struck down by a heart attack on a streetcar platform while en route to
the December anniversary banquet for T. H. Gallaudet. This brutal end to a
fine and remarkable deaf man affected us greatly.

dian in origin. His name is certainly English but perhaps there is some mixture of the two races in his ancestry. He was attentive and helpful to us, although perhaps a little too given to going into bars and tossing back cocktails, which displeased us as much as the abuse of ice water among the puritans. Such extreme contrasts that cannot be balanced have no appeal to the Latin temperament and taste.

Mr. Pach is a very well-known photographer and one of the most striking personalities on Broadway. We shall return to him in a moment. It was Mr. Pach who guided our first steps in New York and brought us to the hotel that Mr. Hodgson had picked out for us. Taking the time after leaving the train to put our luggage in one of the convenient parcel services, better organized and cleaner than the comparable *consignes* in France, from which we could have them brought to the hotel by one of the American Express trucks, we were then ready for the subway.

Mr. Pach had met one of the instructors from the Institution for the Deaf in Rome, New York, Mr. Betts, and he too put himself at our disposal, very pleased to be greeting Frenchmen. He was training as a teacher. We could spend only a few moments together but this was enough to get a very positive impression of him. Mr. Pach communicated with us by lipreading and speech.

We did not have to go down many steps to get the subway. The ceiling arch is almost at ground level, but it is solid. You have to be careful not to jump into the first car that comes along. Here the trains do not shuttle between two end stations, as, for example, on the Vincennes-Maillot line in Paris. There are trains that stop in the middle of the city and others that continue into the suburbs, other still that branch off. Then there are local trains that stop at every station and express trains that shoot through all the intermediary stops and take on and drop off passengers only at certain key points.

You can see all the advantages of the system. The Parisian traveler who was leaving the Bastille station, for example, to go to Étoile would only have to stop at Chatelet, Palais-Royal,

Concorde, and Champs-Élysées, and he would have a car that was not crowded, which would make the trip all the easier. But for the rider who wanted only to get off at Hotel de Ville, too bad, but, with a little patience, you would get there just as quickly as before and still without the crowding. But back to New York. At the rush hour when workers are leaving and returning home, the numbers are staggering. There are people packed together, standing like herrings in a barrel, their arms in the air, hanging from leather straps, while others are seated on the benches that run along each side under the windows. All these people are reading the latest edition of some newspaper, sixteen huge pages with narrow columns in microscopic type yet with whole-page advertisements with Eiffel Tower-sized letters, and cartoons that are sometimes infantile and bizarre. Their dialogue and captions are often incomprehensible to the reader who doesn't know black American slang.

In the space of a trip the newspaper has been leafed through, scanned rather than read. It only costs one cent, thrown to the boys who crisscross the streets, carrying piles of newspapers under their arms with a strength that is surprising for their age. Some even peddle them in the trains. Before their stop, people throw down the paper on their seat. Very few take the trouble to load their hands or pockets down with such a mass of paper. The conductor picks up the abandoned papers and piles of them can be seen at each station. Your eye would be saturated if you tried to read all the New York papers. At the stations at the end of the line, all these papers are gathered up and sold. To whose profit? The employees or the company? But what is sure is that "what goes out from the flute comes back to the drum" (what goes around, comes around). The newsprint goes to pulping then returns to the printing presses and becomes rag again. Perhaps this is why the American printing industry suffers no shortage of paper.

"Hundred and Twenty-First Street, *uptown*!" If we don't forget this number and the idea that we are in the upper part of the city, we are assured of finding our hotel without risking getting lost in the Empire City.

Pach, Spear, and Betts take us to the Hotel Theresa. It is a huge, brand-new building, seventeen stories high. We agree to take two suites of rooms with baths, one for Pilet and Olivier, the other for Graff and me, at three dollars each. It would be impossible to find anything better, more comfortable, or more convenient. Black employees, polite and uniformed, take our bags and lead us up in the elevator. Our rooms are on the fourth floor and we find them attractive. A little freshening up and we rejoin our three guides who take us out to dinner in a huge bar and grill where by a lucky chance we find what was forbidden that Sunday in Hartford: fresh, foaming beer, which makes more appetizing the unknown but well prepared dishes that Mr. Pach, playing the gourmet, recommends to us.

At the Union League

Mr. Hodgson had particularly recommended the Hotel Theresa to us because it is close to the premises where the Deaf Mutes' Union League of New York City meets, just a few steps away on 125th Street.

Pach, Betts, and Spear introduced us. There were lots of people there and we received a cordial welcome. We recognized some of the deaf persons whom we had seen at the Paris Congress in 1912, in particular Mr. Bach, the treasurer, and Mr. Frankenheim. There were others whom I had met in 1893, such as Mr. Capelli, the secretary. Mr. Nuboer, the president, was absent.

While we were getting reacquainted, Mr. Hodgson showed up. Soon, he was up on stage, introducing us with signs of praise. We took turns in signing our speeches of thanks and fraternal sentiment. Then they showed us around the premises. The Union League is on the second floor and has two large rooms separated by the landing. Near the entrance to the first room is a billiard table. A group of chairs stands in front of the stage where addresses are made. There is a table with books, magazines, and newspapers. Against the wall are the offices of the treasurer and secretary. On the walls are series of framed photographs of groups, current and deceased members and benefactors, and past presidents. We notice the portrait of our fellow-countryman, the sculptor Fernand Hamar, along with a menu from the banquet that was offered in his honor by the Union League when he came to dedicate his statue of Rochambeau in Washington.

The second room has another billiard table, cupboards with china, glasses, and cutlery, everything that is needed to have league parties on the premises at certain times of the year. At the rear is a small room, discreet and semi-private, with two gaming tables. People in high sprits are playing cards. There is a similar enthusiasm at the billiard tables. A tax is levied on games and goes to the league.

By a striking coincidence, the Deaf-Mutes' Union League was founded in 1886, the same year as the Ligue pour l'Union Amicale des Sourds-Muets (Fraternal Union League of the Deaf) in Paris. Today it is the Alliance Républicaine des Sourds-Muets (Republican Alliance of the Deaf). Its objectives are about the same: social and recreational, and the intellectual advancement of its members. No individual assistance is foreseen, but rewarding collections are perhaps taken up for members in distress. The membership fee for active members is one dollar and the subsequent monthly fee is fifty cents. Young people aged eighteen to twenty-one are admitted only as associate members, for a fee of thirty cents. The administration of the organization is entrusted to a secretariat composed of a president, two vice presidents, a secretary, and a treasurer, all elected for a one-year term, and a board of nine trustees elected for a term of nine years. The president appoints the vice chairman of the board of trustees, of which he is the ex-officio chairman. The secretary and treasurer receive fifteen dollars a year in remuneration, paid semi-annually. There is also a branch of the secretariat overseeing the investment and banking of funds, a finance committee, and a social committee. Meetings are held the second and fourth Tuesday of each month. General meetings are held in February, April, June, September, and November. The facilities are open Tuesday, Thursday, Saturday, and Sunday from 8:30 to midnight. An anniversary party is held on the third of January each year on League premises. Larger parties, holiday celebrations, dances, congresses, and lectures with moving pictures are held in public places (auditoriums, halls, etc.) in the city. There are also excursions in the summertime. The rent for the League's premises is about $400 per year. This general information will give an idea of how the deaf clubs operate in other cities. In addition to Deaf-Mutes' Division No. 23 of the Union League, there are seven or eight other organizations in New York: the Brooklyn branch of the National Fraternal Society, the Clark Deaf-Mute Athletic Association, the League of Elect Surds, the Men's Club of St. Ann's Church, the Xavier Society, the Knights of de l'Épée (these last two are Roman Catholic), the Alphabet Club, and the Deaf Jews' Society. We shall have an occasion to return to some of these.

The New York Communal Center for the Jewish Deaf

Monday morning, Monsieur Graff and I decided to go out early so that we could, on the one hand, look around the city and, on the other, call on all the agencies, organizations, and businesses of the deaf that were on our path, in a word, integrate our mission of study and observation with the agreeable, especially with what pleases the eye, so important for the deaf person, who may thus console himself over not hearing the harmonies, which are often only cacophonies.

Not too far from 125th Street I knew that the Jewish deaf had their association meeting rooms, at 42–44 115th Street. We got there at nine o'clock to be sure that there would be someone there. The building was in one of the residential districts favored by the Jewish community of New York. There were rows of four-story houses, attractive and well kept, with stone steps in front. Apart from its proud skyscrapers gathered downtown in the business section of the city, with a few others scattered here and there, this entire huge municipal empire is composed of four-story buildings. These buildings are people's homes. Downtown, in the offices and shops people only work.

A marble plaque gives us the information we need. We press a doorbell and a janitor comes and leads us up to the third floor. There is a room with two American-style desks, a great number of filing cabinets, a young woman tapping away at a typewriter, and a young man who gets up to greet us, holding out his hand. This is Harry Futterman. Soon Rabbi A. J. Amateau arrives. They are pleased that we kept the promise I had made in France to visit their organization. Mr. Amateau is a signer, Mr. Futterman a fingerspeller. We chat, they give us detailed information on their activities, we ask each other questions and give frank answers. They show us their files with index cards for all the deaf of New York, both Jews and others. Then we visit the premises. It is amazing that behind such modest walls there lay hidden such useful and important services. Here there are small meeting rooms for women, others for men. There is a library, classrooms for illiterate deaf immigrants who need to learn English, a recreation room with a billiard table, and others for chess and other games. On the second floor there is a huge auditorium with a rather religious look, almost as if it were a synagogue. It is dominated by a high platform, with a lectern resembling an altar. On the wall in back are ritual inscriptions in Hebrew letters. At set hours, religious services are held. At other times, there are signed lectures. The hall can hold about 450 persons. The seating consists of varnished, bent wooden chairs. In the basement there is a hall for parties and receptions, theatrical presentations, and dances. There is also a spacious gymnasium with all kinds of athletic equipment, showers, and a small dormitory for deaf immigrants who are temporarily without lodging. Behind the buildings is a basketball court and a closed garden. The purchase of the three buildings was made possible by anonymous gifts and the necessary remodeling was then carried out. All this cost about $52,000. If one takes into account the high cost of real estate in New York, I consider that this was not too expensive and that it was advantageous to buy all three buildings and to change them so ingeniously into a well integrated complex. The Parisian promoters of a Foyer des Sourds-Muets (Deaf Center) should perhaps take some inspiration from this model and buy a fairly spacious city building that is already in place, then take down the inner walls and stairways and carry out the necessary modifications. This would certainly proceed more rapidly than constructing a new building. But it is possible that what is easy in New York, where the engineer takes precedence over the architect, would be difficult in Paris. Still, it's worth thinking about.

The agency, the Society for the Welfare of the Jewish Deaf, has been in existence for six years. It is supported by membership fees and by philanthropy. Its income in 1916 was about $4,480 and its expenses $5,970. Salary costs for the executive secretary, his assistant, a clerk, the teachers for the classes in religious instruction and for immigrants amounted to more than $9,000. This left them assets of only just over $1,000. But efforts are being made to create a maintenance fund. The president of the society is Abraham Erlanger, a rich industrialist and great philanthropist who has interested himself in deaf people of his religion in a practical and generous way. It is greatly thanks to him that this agency exists, that it was able to weather its initial difficulties, and is now in the process of stabilizing itself. Its benefactor's name will live on in the hearts of the Jewish deaf and others, for, as I shall go on to show, the activities of the society profit the deaf of other religions as well. A number of prominent Jews support the work of the society and among these are some Jewish deaf such as Samuel Frankenheim and Marcus L. Kenner and others whose name I do not know. The vice president is Mr. Leo Sulzberger; the honorary treasurers, Mr. Norman and Mr. Cohen; the treasurers, Mr. Sidney and Erlanger; the executive secretary is Rabbi A. J. Amateau. Among the trustees whose names I recognized are Dr. D. de Sola Pool who has dealt with deaf issues in articles that have come to my attention, and Mr. Isidore Monteliore Levy. A family with the same name has always been prominent in Liège in its generous support of the deaf association of that city. A number of specialized groups are affiliated with the society. They are made up of deaf people and are administered by the deaf. Thus they have a Hebrew Congregation of the Deaf of which Marcus Kenner is the president; the Sisterhood of the Hebrew Deaf, whose president is Mrs. J. A. Cohen. The religious activity of the Jewish deaf in New York is perhaps unique in the world. In European countries, at any case in France, what we might call the benefits of Jewish religion are ordinarily not extended to the deaf of that faith. Although viewing this from some distance, I have long called attention to this fact and deplored it. Yet deaf French Jews are fairly numerous, especially in Paris, and I know at least one whose brother is a rabbi and knows sign language and could be very helpful to the deaf of his religion. In neglecting the spiritual needs of its children without hearing, the Jewish community of Paris gives evidence of a negligence that is all the less pardonable when we recall that one of the great precursors in the education of the deaf, along with the Abbé de l'Épée, was Jacob Rodrigues Pereire, who was, moreover, an ardent defender of the Jewish cause.

If in New York and other American cities people have given realistic and effective thought to the matter, it is certainly because the Jewish deaf are more numerous, that many come from wealthy families and, after exposure to the American educational system, have been able to draw intellectual and material advantage from their children deprived of hearing. In addition, marriage between cousins or between persons more distantly related, which is more or less imposed by a strict rule not to marry outside the ancestral religious community, these consanguineous unions, more than in case of other ethnic groups, seem to generate substantial numbers of deaf children. There are often two, three, or four children in one branch of the same family and just as many in another. Thus, in Paris, I knew a brother and sister who had male and female cousins in Germany who were also deaf, with additional deaf relatives in the United States. If Alexander Graham Bell foresaw the formation of a deaf species of humans, it would be among these exclusively Jewish marriages and families that he might see the first glimpse of it rather than in marriages among deaf persons without other close relationship.

No matter, the American Jewish philanthropists who see to the religious, moral, intellectual, and social needs of the Jewish deaf deserve the admiration and gratitude of all true friends of humanity. They give true proof of their civilized status. What we have seen of the silent Jewish world more than proves that their sacrifices have not been in vain. Perfect gentlemen, capable of managing their own affairs; credentialed workers, rather than parasites living off the investments of their parents as in France; intelligent and gracious women with whom it is a pleasure to engage in a light flirtation to add to one's store of souvenirs—this is what we met in New York among this community which in Europe would have been treated as undesirables. As for numbers, many come from Poland or Russia, saved by their mothers from the savage anti-Semitic pogroms that were in place there under the earlier czarist regime. As much as the Americans of older stock, they are an honor to their race and fully justify the respect of which they are the object.

In fact, the principal objective of the Society for the Welfare of the Jewish Deaf is to provide industrial training and find places for the unemployed Jewish deaf of New York City. Its labor office for the deaf is the first to have been founded in the world. I called attention to it at the Chicago Congress of 1893. Another such office has recently been set up in Minnesota, the first to have official status, and which came about thanks to the efforts of the president of the National Association of the Deaf, Jay Cook Howard. Now, congress in Washington is studying a bill that would create a national office and thus have greater resources and effectiveness. But it was truly the labor office for the Jewish deaf that paved the way.

Mr. Amateau took the initiative in this regard, and he showed the skill of a practical sociologist. In any case, he has been an admirable administrator and has achieved the hoped-for results.

In his annual report, President Abraham Erlanger could state with the satisfaction of a good conscience, "I am told that in this city there is not one Jewish deaf-mute out of work."

Every agency worthy of the name keeps statistics of its activity and Mr. Amateau would have been at fault if he had not published his figures. Here is what we were able to extract from his report for 1916.

	1914	1915	1916
Number of positions sought	170	105	64
Positions about to be assumed	21	3	0
Positions declined	0	12	0
Pending at the end of the year	19	0	0
Positions found	196	192	85

You will note that the number of places sought decreased from year to year and that all searches were successful. In 1914, of 130 persons placed, there are some that were found work from three to eight times. In 1916, fifty-one persons were placed directly and stayed with their job, and only two changed their place of work four times before finding a situation that both they and their employers found satisfactory.

In the figure for 1916 we note sixty-one Jews and three non-Jews. Thus we can state that the agency is not simply charitable in its function, but also social in that it serves the needs of those beyond the bounds of faith.

This figure breaks down into fifty-one men and thirteen women, of which total seven were married and fifty-seven single. I do not have an exact figure for the number of Jewish deaf in New York City. I am told that there are about 10,000 deaf residents of which 2,500 to 3,000 are of the Jewish faith. Whether this is an exaggeration or not, it nonetheless gives an idea of what the relative numbers might be.

The report also gives the average weekly salary of those who found work through the office. I see that a linotype operator earns twenty-six dollars, an engraver twenty-five dollars, compositors ten dollars, which is rather little. Many other jobs pay seven dollars a week and those who had learned no trade were obliged to settle for more modest wages.

The report also works up a rather unexpected bit of statistics. It makes a comparison between the average earnings of a deaf-Mute and a deaf person who speaks and reads lips. For 1914 the report cites ninety-nine persons in the latter category who earned $11.25 on average. Wages for seventeen persons who signed and also read lips were $9. The fifty-nine workers who only signed earned $7.75.

But I think that this is just the ingenuity of the statistician! No doubt, a deaf person who can make himself understood in speech and who can read lips will always be valued higher than someone who obliges others to have recourse to pencil and paper to make themselves understood. But for many employers this handicap creates no awkwardness. What they prize above all is vocational competence. A skillful deaf-mute who masters his craft will be of greater value to the paymaster and will receive his due.

I know deaf-mutes whose education by the old method was less than elementary but who have industrial skills well beyond the ordinary and who pocket four times as much as rough-voiced stammerers whose vocational training was poorly focused on a long, painful, and fruitless effort to teach speech.

Mr. Amateau's statistics prove rather that by introducing the oral method schools have improved their vocational training and have produced better workers. It could also demonstrate that pupils who are trained in small oral schools, where there are no vocational classes, have had to do their apprenticeship with hearing people, which has had the advantage of giving them a sure mastery of their craft.

But the office, which has undertaken a systematic study of the working conditions of the deaf, as in a laboratory, the report states, has noted that of the 339 cases with which it has been concerned over the space of three years, two-thirds or 225 persons had left school before the completion of their course of study. This is a real discovery, indeed. For, in fact, almost all these young people had been unable to keep their jobs for any length of time. This has led to the duplication, triplication, and more of the work done for a single candidate for employment, a tremendous expenditure of energy to find him a suitable place or find him better employment. Without support, subsidy, or encouragement, I have myself experienced the trouble one must take to find a living for some of the lesser products of the national institution in Paris, in particular tailors and typographers.

This agency has a review, *The Jewish Deaf,* which appears monthly in a twenty-page octavo format. It is composed with artistry and printed by deaf workers under the auspices of The Jewish Deaf Publishing Company, part of the printing operation of Marcus L. Kenner. This is one of the best magazines we have. I have admired it particularly because in addition to news and articles about the deaf it has been concerned, much more than other publications, with defending the right of the deaf to employment. It led the campaign to improve their vocational training and to get employers to recognize their production potential. In this undertaking, Harry Futterman is Rabbi Amateau's useful auxiliary.

The organization bears a heavy financial burden in assuring the publication of the review, since the financial report for 1916 reveals that it cost almost $1,000 and brought in only $130, the subscription fee being only one dollar per year. But the review is primarily distributed as a form of propaganda and is circulated free of charge to supporters and other prominent persons that it seeks to influence.

This publicity is very useful not only for the Jewish deaf but for deaf people in general. The expense is then a sound invest-ment and the effect is far-reaching.

Since I asked for a copy of the June issue, which had been sent to me when I was at sea, I had the pleasant surprise of see-ing that the lead article for the month dealt with the industrial training of the deaf and gave some space to ideas of my own about apprenticeships outside school that I had presented to the congresses in Paris, Chicago, Liège, and Rome. I thanked Rabbi Amateau who had undertaken the translation and Mr. Futterman. It seemed that both took my side in the matter: to devote school time to the exclusive task of instruction; to put pupils who had reached the age for apprenticeship in the company of young hearing persons in public vocational schools or in private workshops; to permit the schools to offer shop training in crafts and trades readily accessible to the greatest number, i.e., shoemaking, cabinetmaking, locksmithing, etc.

When it was founded, the Jewish Society set up a workshop for the use of some deaf persons (about 2 percent of their total) who had proven incapable of performing useful work elsewhere and whom employers had turned down. There was a certain risk in continuing to recommend them, for their lack of aptitude might suggest that all the deaf were in the same boat, since there is a tendency to extrapolate from the particular to the general. They were then taken off the labor market and given places under the supervision of the society. They were chiefly occupied in printing signs on calico. But in 1916 a fire destroyed the building where space for the shop had been rented. In the meantime these deaf workers had shown some improvement and it turned out that it was possible to place them with good salaries. The administration then judged it unnecessary to set up a similar workshop on the new premises. The infrequent cases that later occurred, only three or four, were treated individually and were referred to understanding employers who placed no great demands on them.

The office makes its findings known to the institutions for the deaf on the old principle that an ounce of prevention is worth a pound of cure. In fact, it is through the experience gained from observing working conditions and seeking placements that it has proved possible to improve vocational training.

Above I noted the existence of classrooms for deaf immigrants. In charge is a remarkable deaf person who uses speech, a proofreader with one of the large presses for art catalogs, Mr. Samuel Kohn. You can imagine the usefulness of classes like this for those who arrive from the Russian provinces completely ignorant of the English language. The class meets two times a week. There is an advanced course which also meets twice weekly for those who want to improve their English. The average number of pupils in these classes is twelve.

The society also performs other useful services. Mr. Amateau's assistance is often requested in court to serve as interpreter. The society has plans to set up a medical clinic for the deaf and their children.

American immigrations laws are, as we know, very stringent. They once proscribed the admission of deaf immigrants with no other reason given. But it is thanks to the efforts of this society that this unjustified exclusion has been modified. Now all deaf persons who otherwise meet the health conditions that are required are admitted provided that, like hearing immigrants, they can establish that they can read, understand, and write at least their native language.

Before we left, Mr. Amateau received us in his residence on the upper floor and introduced us to Mrs. Amateau, a gracious and cultivated lady. She is Parisian and was born near the Bastille. This made it all the more pleasant to present our respects and to congratulate her for being such a devoted and valuable collaborator of her husband.

The Church of the Deaf

I had already visited Saint Ann's Church for the Deaf in 1893. It was located in downtown New York and was rather small and narrow. But now it has been moved uptown, to 511 West 148th Street, and has been totally reconstructed.

When we visited it for the first time it was already evening. Nothing distinguishes it from the other buildings on the street, unless it is the archway topped by a gothic cross over the doorway and the plaque announcing the function of the building. The church has three stories. The windows of the first floor are high, deep, and arched. Stained glass shines from the frames. Higher up, the square middle class widows suggest a residence. The effect is rather bizarre and the architect could have done a better job.

We enter a huge vestibule divided by a long, high, accordion-style partition that allows the hall to be divided in two for smaller meetings or left as one large one for bigger assemblies. In fact, it would be a violation of the holy precincts to have secular conferences in the chapel itself. They are here instead. There is another hall in the basement with smaller rooms for tea, games, and conversation opening off it. This part of the building is called the Guild House.

The chapel is wide, quite deep, lit by stained glass windows. The central altar is simple and austere with a cross flanked by two candles and two candleholders with five branches, placed on a white cloth where alpha and omega are visible, the beginning and the end of all things. An embrasure with two false Doric columns is situated above and tries to give a bit of majesty to the nudity of the walls. On the right is a small baptismal font. There is a lectern for a large Bible. And that is all. If I add that the benches are of varnished wood, stacked one on top of another, you will understand just how sober an impression it gives.

The only ornamentation is on the left side wall where we saw a marble bas relief of the Rev. Thomas Gallaudet, the work of the deaf sculptor Hannan, who studied in Paris with Paul Choppin and Leon Morice. This is a fine work.

But, everything has not yet been completed. Bit by bit, as new resources become available, the furnishings and decorations are being improved. A great deal has already been accomplished and the congregation is more comfortably and spaciously accommodated than in the past.

I was not informed what it cost to construct the church nor what its operating expenses might be. The reports that were turned over to me did not mention the subject. We were received by the Rev. John H. Keiser, an oral deaf missionary, the coadjutant of the Rev. Dr. John Chamberlain, director general of the mission, who was absent. Rev. Keiser was kind enough to receive us in his residence, one floor above, and introduced his charming wife. He made us the gift of a photograph taken by Pach. He is an outstanding oral member of the deaf community, very devoted to his flock and seeking all possible means for their advancement. In this he is an admirable deputy to the Rev. Chamberlain, who has devoted himself to deaf New Yorkers and others for almost forty-four years. Rev. Chamberlain participated in our celebration of the bicentenary of the Abbé de l'Épée. Under a slightly cool exterior he has a heart of gold.

The mission has more than a religious purpose. The pastors also assist members of their flock in finding employment, they call on the sick, and distribute assistance to the needy. The work is both Christian and socially useful.

The parishioners of St. Ann of the Deaf have formed various fraternal and athletic associations. The largest of these is the St. Ann's Men's Club, which has a kind of general supervisory function.

In the course of our visit we had the pleasure of making the acquaintance of Dr. J. Schuyler Long, who had left Hartford before our arrival. He is a former student of Gallaudet College, a teacher, writer, and talented poet, and the author of a remarkable dictionary of sign language, the only one of its kind in the world. I hardly need to say that Chamberlain, Keiser, and Long are all expert signers.

The mission is also in charge of the Gallaudet Home for the Aged and Infirm Deaf in Wappinger's Falls near Poughkeepsie. I had visited it in 1893. On this occasion, however, we did not have the time. If we had, I would have seen the new building, much larger than the old one, which had been destroyed by fire in 1900.

My study of the home for the aged deaf in Pennsylvania will give an idea of what these particularly American institutions are like. Let me begin by saying that the revenues for the Gallaudet Home were just over $11,000 and the expenses slightly above this figure, leaving a slight deficit. But the maintenance fund has almost $200,000 and the institution will be well able to meet future challenges.

In 1916, the clergymen Chamberlain and Keiser celebrated 224 Sunday or holiday services, twenty-two weekday services, seventy-five public communions and nine private ones, twelve baptisms, of which seven were of adults, thirty-three confirmations, four marriages and nine funerals.

As with all churches, St. Ann's is supported by the collection and by gifts. The church's revenues in 1916 were just under $4,000 and its outlays about $1,000 more than that, chiefly in the form of aid to the ill and needy. The salary of the general administrator, who is Rev. Chamberlain, is just under $2,000 and that of the missionary, Rev. Keiser, about half that. So, the church is operating with a deficit. But luckily there is a revolving fund, so that this can be accommodated.

The New York church is under the direction of a board of trustees with twenty-five members, over which the bishop of New York, the Right Rev. David H. Greer, presides. He is assisted by two vice chairmen, the Rev. A. H. Judge and M. E. A. Hodgson. Like the editor-in-chief of *The Deaf Mutes' Journal*, there are other deaf persons on the board, such as Messrs. Fox and Nuboer.

The general administrator John Chamberlain is the second in command to the Rev. Thomas Gallaudet. He is assisted by Miss Virginia B. Gallaudet, one of the daughters of the founder, and the Rev. J. H. Keiser. A deaf lay reader, Mr. Ch. Q. Mann, also provides auxiliary services to the pastors.

Almost all these clergymen are products of the oral method. They have completed serious theological studies and were ordained as clergymen in their church after a special and quite rigorous examination by their bishops. In acknowledging the right of educated and enlightened deaf persons of irreproachable habits the right within the religious community to instruct and sustain their fellows of like condition, the Episcopal Church, like the Methodist Church, which also has deaf clergy, among whom Rev. Hasenstab in Chicago, has shown itself more advanced on

the path of the Lord than the Roman Catholic Church, which
has always had difficulties in admitting the deaf to holy orders,
and permits them only as lay brothers and congregationist nuns.

The collective name of the church is The Church Mission
to Deaf-Mutes and it is now in its 45th year of existence. It
was founded in 1872 by the Rev. Thomas Gallaudet, one of
the sons of Thomas Hopkins Gallaudet and the brother of
Edward Miner Gallaudet. Thomas Gallaudet twice attended the
Paris congress and in 1893 gave a very warm welcome to the
French delegation.

He has been the driving force behind the creation of similar
churches or missions for the deaf in all the United States. They
are part of the Episcopalian Church and beyond New York there
are twelve member churches and pastors. These are J. H. Cloud
in Saint Louis, C. Orvis Dantzer in Philadelphia, O. J. Whildin
in Baltimore, Mr. Van Allen in Utica, Franklin C. Smielau in
Williamsport, George F. Flick in Chicago, J. M. Koehler in
Kansas City, G. H. Hefflon in Hartford, B. A. Allabough in Ohio,
Herbert Merril in Washington, H. L. Tracy in Baton Rouge, and
Clarence W. Charles in Columbus.

To these should be added those who are at rest in Paradise:
the Rev. H. W. Syle, the founder of the church in Philadelphia,
Thomas Gallaudet, that of the church in New York, Job Turner,
Francis Clerc, one of the hearing sons of Laurent Clerc, Searing, and A. W. Mann. The Reverends Turner and Mann participated in the Paris Congress of 1889.

Samuel Frankenheim

At our meeting at the Union League we had expressed a wish
to see New York by night, the entertainment and other celebrated
areas, the brilliantly lit streets, and so on. At once, someone came
to our assistance. This was Mr. Samuel Frankenheim, a real gentleman by education and manner. He was a member of the delegation to the bicentenary celebration in honor of the Abbé de

l'Épée in 1912 and it is he who staged the impromptu banquet for the American deaf at the Hotel Regina on the rue de Rivoli. After having served as treasurer for the fundraising committee for the monument to the Abbé de l'Épée, he had succeeded the Rev. Cloud as president of the Union League when the latter was called to the presidency of the NAD. Mr. Frankenheim is an active member of the deaf community. He is on the board of several associations, among others that for the welfare of the Jewish deaf. On several occasions he has been chairman or president. With his financial acumen he has undertaken to introduce deaf subscribers to mutual insurance societies, personal loans, savings stamp ventures, and patriotic associations.

He received us in his home, well situated on one of the new streets off Central Park. It was a jewel of a bachelor apartment, comfortably furnished and artistically decorated, betraying the intellectual tastes of its owner. Down to the kitchen and pantry consigned to the care of a maid, everything was ideally organized for a bachelor who wanted comfort and peace while pursuing an active and studious life.

Mr. Frankenheim's father had also been a patron of the deaf. For this reasons his portrait graces the walls of the Union League. He came to New York as a poor immigrant from a town in Germany and made a fortune in business. During his lifetime, as is the case with all Americans even those who have become rich, he made his son work to learn how to make his own living.

Samuel Frankenheim was employed by a famous photographer. Today, he has remained an amateur photographer and the group photographs and panoramas that he has shot in the course of his travels, particularly to Paris, Mexico, and in the American West, are luminous, with suggestive immediacy and a lively sense of the picturesque.

In the course of the evening he showed us the most interesting entertainment spots in New York and he was most generous toward his French guests. He would not allow us to pay for anything and he invited us to a Chinese dinner with very expensive dishes. Chinese cuisine is famous in New York and there are numerous restaurants of this kind where one eats unique and refined food, which however can initially be a bit disconcerting to the palate and stomach.

I would like to be able to give an impression of Times Square lit up as if it were day from the pavement to the rooftops, with its theaters, music halls, cinemas, restaurants with orchestras and dancing, its illuminated signs, huge, curious, moving, some running along the elevated railroad, rolling out advertising in garish lettering, making up unexpected turns of phrase, with animated cartoon characters and crude humor. But this would take me too far from our specific subject. I would only note that New Yorkers have a taste not only for dancing past midnight but also for watching people dance. Every fashionable restaurant has its chorus line of dancing girls, pretty and agile, who shake, spin, and kick in fantastic moves and steps, and charming changes of costume, but all very chaste and tasteful. In this vast metropolis the art of Terpsichore has passed to cult status.

Samuel Frankenheim served as our guide on the following days as well. He took us to see the Statue of Liberty illuminating the world from the center of the most beautiful area imaginable. He dealt with Cook's Travel Agency to get our tickets for Niagara, Toronto, and Cleveland. We repeated our expressions of gratitude. The eminent president of the committee for the monument to the Abbé de l'Épée thus displayed the affection that he, as a true democrat and complete American, had for France.

The New York Institution

Its common name is the Washington Heights Institution, being situated on the height of land where Fort Washington was constructed. It now occupies 90 Fort Washington Avenue at the corner of 163rd Street. It is quite some distance from downtown and lies beyond the attractive promenade of Riverside Drive along the Hudson River, which is dominated by the impressive tomb of General Grant. The institution itself lies along the river front. I seem to remember that in 1893, when I came for the first time, the lawns ran down to the water's edge. Now a public thoroughfare open to wheeled traffic and lined with a grill fence cuts the property in two, perhaps as the result of some municipal requirement. But along the edge of the grounds, canoes and small craft belonging to the institution are still moored.

In 1893 the water of the Hudson shone under the sun, mirroring the distant beauty of the landscape. Today, it is brownish under a soot-darkened rain whose vapors slowly, and as if regretfully, drift off toward Europe and its tragic and uncertain future.

We had agreed with Mr. Hodgson that we would visit the institution the morning of Wednesday, July 21. Pilet and Olivier had arrived first, and Graff and I brought up the rear. The principal of the institution, the eminent Mr. Enoch Henry Currier, had been alerted to our visit. Although he had an appointment elsewhere, he was kind enough to wait for us and gave us a friendly welcome. A master of sign language, like all principals of American schools, he had no trouble conversing with us. I had already met him in 1893 and he was still erect, smiling, and hearty under his head of white hair. Alas! Only a few days later during the heat wave of August he was to die suddenly at his country home and then be buried on his birthday.

A good man, great teacher of the deaf, and energetic defender of their interests, Enoch Henry Currier will live on in the memory of all American deaf. And the deaf of other countries will perhaps some day learn to venerate his immortal name as much as that of Gallaudet among the names of our great intellectual and social liberators.

Enoch Henry Currier made the New York Institution the first military college for the deaf in the world. And he successfully taught his pupils to perform military band music in the open air. In addition, he has achieved practical developments in the auditory reeducation of those who have some residual hearing.

We should not smile at military training for the deaf. In fact, this is really nothing absolutely new. In my time, the national institution for the deaf in Paris had us carry out exercises and march, carrying wooden rifles, to the sound of a drum. It was a very good complement to gymnastic exercises and gave us a taste for rapid and correct, tireless and healthy walking, the sense for movement and discipline. They could have added target shooting since most deaf persons have a well developed faculty of sight and become excellent marksmen. The exploits of deaf hunters are all the evidence you need.

I would imagine that rather similar principles must have guided Mr. Currier in his thorough and consistent practice of military drills. Pupils wear a military-style uniform and all movement is carried out with military precision. Even when they go to the washrooms, then to the dining hall, to chapel and to class, the pupils have to march in ranks, stop as a single man, look after the same details at the same time with precise movements: sitting down, standing up, grouping and dispersing, all strictly on a visual command or at the sound of a trumpet. The objective, according to the report, is to predispose each pupil to a positive attitude, to prompt and cheerful obedience to teachers, to give them the powers of attention and concentration, and an aptitude to take initiatives. The effect of the concentrated rhythmical

Cadets at Fanwood

movements is clearly positive, if one is to judge from the stylish, free, and easy movements of the pupils whom we met in the course of our visit.

In addition to the principal, the teaching staff is composed of eight teachers and twenty-six male and female instructors. Several of these belong to the section that teaches speech articulation, lipreading, and aural education. There is also a kindergarten section and transitional classes, which prepare pupils for regular elementary school. It is remarkable, in the American approach to early childhood education and in particular to the difficult and demanding task of teaching the mute to speak, that there is such heavy reliance on female teachers. They make up the majority of teachers of the deaf.

Ten trades are taught at the school: printing and typography; cabinet- and furnituremaking; tailoring; baking; sign painting; making dresses, shirts, underclothes, and coats; cooking, gardening. The principal object of study is the English language with emphasis on phraseology, sentences, narrative and descriptions, dialogues and letters. Elementary education also includes arithmetic, geography, history, natural science, comportment and morals, civics, health and physiology—in short, the essentials of what every man and woman should know. There are thity-one oral classes and nine manual classes for those who cannot profit from the pure oral method. Some of the latter have been put under the direction of deaf instructors, among whom Thomas Francis Fox (M.A., D.Litt.) and William G. Jones (M.A.), that is, signing and the finger-alphabet are permitted in the classroom, while instruction emphasizes writing and lipreading. There is also a class for those who are blind and deaf.

The ratio of pupils taught orally to those taught manually is not constant and can vary with the subject matter. The teaching of music starts with the very real fact that the deaf perceive musical vibrations and this has proven useful in the acquisition of speech and in perfecting enunciation. It also appears to improve the aural receptivity of the hard of hearing. In fact, through the practice of musical instruments, in particular woodwinds and brass, which require the control of the breath, the deaf pupil acquires a sense of moderation and harmony and can eventually learn to shade his voice. The hard of hearing have made progress in the sense that such regular exposure sharpens their auditory perception. For the rest, the reader is advised to consult Currier's newspaper articles and pamphlets on the subject. What is certain, I have been told, and what I have read in the deaf press as well as newspapers, is that the concerts given by these deaf musicians charm the ears of their audience and have been extremely successful. "The band played patriotic airs of all nations most acceptably," writes Mrs. Sarah Harvey Porter, in the *American Annals of the Deaf.*

Mr. Currier introduced us to the military drill instructor, William H. van Tassell. He is also the steward and bookkeeper, a very tall and cordial man. He is an excellent administrator and is the principal's right hand. Since our visit he has been promoted to the assistant principalship.

Obliged to leave, Mr. Currier presented his apologies. He gave us a copy of the current annual report for the past school year, the ninety-ninth in the series. This is a 112-page publication, with an extremely attractive layout and typography, printed on glossy paper by the pupils in the print shop under the direction of their teacher, Mr. Hodgson. Drawings executed by the pupils alternate attractively with the print and original decorative elements, while numerous excellent photographs of candid scenes, views of buildings, and classrooms amaze the incredulous reader who might have wondered about the progress being made at the New York Institution.

In the past a French teacher once came here to complete his training. This was Leon Vaïsse who became the principal of the national institution and brought to it a number of useful innovations which, had it not been for our traditional resistance to change and his lack of better support, would have led to very positive results.

It is very desirable that French teachers visit the American institutions, even that they take classes there and learn the methods. Most of them would gain a better conception of things, would learn how to make a more reasoned and moderate application of methods, or rather of method, for there can in truth be only one, the method that takes into account all the means available to the pupils to achieve better human results, which is to realize the good of the individual while adapting him and her to the social profit of the collectivity.

We toured various parts of the building with Mr. Hodgson as guide and for a part of the time in the company of Mr. Van Tassell. But, to tell the truth, to make a proper visit to an institution of this importance, one would have to be there when it was functioning with all its intense life and not during the summer holidays. One would need to come back several times, at different times of the day, or live there for a week in order to absorb fully its specific essence. Then one would be able to bring back a wealth of interesting observations, and write a detailed book on it alone, a book that would be of great importance for French special education and for the general improvement of the lot of the deaf.

The educational furnishings, the layout of the speech classrooms, that of the advanced classes, some of which do not have a single desk, just chairs with a wide board on the right where you can write or take notes, this and other details would warrant a full description. But our visit was too rapid and I took only a few mental notes as is my habit.

Everything here was on a large scale, spacious, bright, clean and proper, and very comfortable.

In the hallway of the administration wing there is an exhibit of works of art won by the cadets in competition with hearing pupils from other colleges. On the walls are paintings and photographs, portraits of benefactors of the school and prominent teachers, including the Peets, Senior and Junior, and Currier himself. Some have been executed by the celebrated deaf American painter John Carlin, who was a former pupil of the institution and who regularly went to France during the Second Empire at the time of Ferdinand Berthier, who was his friend.

The Institution has 482 pupils, 300 boys and 182 girls. Of these, 250 receive state support and 134 support from their municipalities. One hundred ninety-eight of the pupils are deaf from birth; forty-nine went deaf between the ages of one and two; six at age eight; three at age fourteen; seventy-two at unrecorded ages. Cerebro-spinal meningitis is the illness which struck the greatest number of individuals (ninety-nine) after congenital deafness (198). Then come cerebral fever (thirty-five), scarlet fever (twenty-two), flux (twenty-three), falls (twenty-one), negative results of vaccinations (two), eczema (one), and so on.

The pupils have formed a Fanwood Literary Association, after the popular name for the property on which the school is located. It is made up of the members of the academic stream, the principal, and the teachers. The principal is its adviser and the head teacher of the academic classes is the president. The first vice president is chosen by the pupils. In 1916 it was Jean-Paul Gruet, who is mentioned elsewhere in this report, and his deputy also had a name of Romance origin, Santo y Guinta.

The objectives of this society are to stimulate the literary efforts of the pupils, to interest them in language, to encourage them to treat lofty subjects, and to develop an appreciation for study and reading. The society has its own special library. Lectures are given in sign language and some recent topics have been international law and American diplomacy; the future of post-war Europe; the United States armed forces, war preparations and peace; the tricentenary of Shakespeare. For the last-named, the pupils staged the following plays at their Saturday evening dramatic performances: *Cymbeline, King Lear, The Merchant of Venice, As You Like It*, and *Much Ado About Nothing*.

There are also athletic associations for football and basketball. In fact, in addition to the military training of which Mr. van Tassell is in charge and the open air band led by Mr. Edwards, there are two directors of physical education, Altenderfer and Matthews.

The advanced or academic class is an advanced manual class under the direction of the learned deaf teacher Thomas Francis

Fox. He has five pupils, all boys. There are eight oral grammar classes that have an average of eight to twelve pupils each, some composed of both boys and girls. There are eleven intermediary classes, seven primary classes, and eleven pre-school classes.

The course of study is of five years, but may be extended to eight, nine, or eleven. Pupils who successfully pass their final examinations receive a graduating diploma. In 1916, twenty-six pupils received diplomas after eight years of study, two after eleven years. Three were recommended by the commissioner of education to enter an advanced class with renewed public support. One of these was the lad with the French name, Jean-Paul Gruet.

It should be noted that among the awards that are made at the end of the academic year, several have been offered by deaf persons or by organizations of deaf adults—thus, the Henry Jansen Haight prize for painting, the Manhattan Literary Association of Deaf-Mutes' prize for printing, that of the Holywood Fraternity of Deaf-Mutes for girls, that of the League of Elect Surds and of the Fraternal Society for graduating pupils. The Deanistown Prize for excellence in English composition was won by Jean-Paul Gruet. Hurrah! Would he understand what was said to him in the language of his ancestors: *Je suis fier de toi, mon fils!* "I am proud of you, my boy!" The same Jean-Paul Gruet carried off the first prize in art, which was offered to the institution by a French woman, Madame Jumel, who, according to what I have read somewhere, was prominent at the court of Napoleon III and went into exile in America after the fall of the Empire, but this story may not stand up to scrutiny. In any case, this elderly lady, who was living in the neighborhood, became interested in the deaf youngsters that she saw out on walks and bequeathed a portion of her fortune to the institution.

The financial situation of the latter shows just over $152,000 in income and about $158,000 in expenses, resulting in a deficit of about $5,700. This has been the consequence of the rise in the cost of food, which was in part offset by the capital fund of the Institution. The principal part of operating revenue comes from state subsidies in support of the pupils. The revolving fund amounts to $1,115,475. It is made up chiefly of bequests and special gifts, and may not be spent on operating costs, except those for the maintenance and repair of buildings.

The trustees of the institution are twenty-four prominent citizens of New York, lawyers, bankers, clergymen, businessmen, army officers, brokers, and investors. The board, under the presidency of Charles Augustus Stoddard, is constituted in three groups and seven committees: executive, financial, bylaws and regulations, revolving fund, library, and nominating committees. There is also a committee of female patrons of the school.

The New York Institution celebrated its centenary this year, along with the school in Hartford, on 15 April. One might think that the two schools contend over seniority as the first American school for the deaf. But this is in fact not the case. In the "Recital" that he read at the Commemorative Exercises, Enoch Henry Currier laid things out in impartial fashion. The Hartford Institution was established in 1816 and the one in New York opened its doors in 1818. And, by a curious coincidence that rebounds to the honor of France and the French deaf community, just as it was the deaf Frenchman Laurent Clerc who assisted Thomas Hopkins Gallaudet in Hartford, it was another deaf Frenchman who, at some distance, inspired the foundation of the school in New York. This was F. Gard of Bordeaux, who had been a pupil of Saint-Sernin. But let's pick up Currier's thread. The real founder of the New York Institution was the Reverend John Stanford, a teacher and clergyman, who on his arrival in New York in 1786 opened an academy. In 1807 he discovered some deaf immigrants in a hostel whose plight touched him. He dreamed of creating a classroom for them with a young teacher and slates so that their education might be carried out with the aid of writing. This was the first American school for the deaf. A learned friend of Stanford, Dr. Samuel L. Mitchell, devised their motto: *Vicaria Manus Linguae*, the hand replaces the tongue. This figures on the seal of the institution in an inscription above the letter A of the finger alphabet. But changes in the administration of the hostel forced the closure of the classes. Yet the objective was not abandoned. Americans gradually became aware of the efforts of European educators of the deaf and the names of de l'Épée, Sicard, Braidwood, and Watson were associated with some sparse information on the systems in use in France and England. The children of the wealthy were being sent to England. One of these, Charles Green, was the son of the famous author Francis Green. The author visited Thomas Braidwood in Edinburgh. Enthusiastically, he praised his method of teaching articulation and lipreading in the journal, *The New York Medical Repository*. This article had considerable influence on the foundation of the New York Institution.

At the same time, three deaf members of the Bolling family (which also counted the wife of President Woodrow Wilson among its members), wealthy residents of Virginia, had been entrusted to Braidwood and had returned from Europe remarkably well educated. The father of one of them, Colonel William Bolling, wanted his fellow citizens to profit by these positive developments. He invited the grandson of the Scottish educator, Thomas Braidwood, to open a school in Baltimore in 1812. Unfortunately, this young man, however skillful a teacher he may have been, spent the funds entrusted to him on alcohol and loose living. The school was closed, but Thomas Braidwood opened another in New York toward the end of the same year. However his eccentric life style did not change and the poor man eventually died of alcoholism.

But his venture had attracted public attention, among others that of Dr. Samuel Akerly, who became the physician, secretary, and principal of the future institution, and also the author of the first practical work on the education of the deaf, *Elementary Exercises for the Deaf and Dumb*. In 1816 while these developments were in progress, William Lee returned from Bordeaux, where he had been the American consul, with a circular letter from F. Gard, the distinguished pupil of Saint-Sernin. (At the same time there had been an American pupil at the Royal Institution for Deaf-Mutes in Paris. Was this the son or a relative of the same William Lee?) This letter, written in excellent English,

for Gard had studied the language, was addressed to the "Philanthropists of the United States" and contained the offer that
he himself would become the teacher of the American deaf.

Mr. Lee hastened to convene a number of prominent people among whom the Rev. Standford, Samuel Mitchell, General
Jonas Mapes, and Dr. Akerly. They discussed possibilities for the
education of the deaf. Other meetings were held at Tammany
Hall to find the ways and means to establish a school. First, they
wanted to know the number of young deaf persons of a suitable
age to be admitted. The population of New York City was then
120,000. They determined that the ratio of deaf to be about one
in 1,818. Mr. Currier informs me that this ratio has continued
down to the present.

New Yorkers were at this stage of discussions and meetings
in 1817 when they learned that an institution, a real functioning school, had been created in Hartford, in the state of Connecticut, in May of 1816 by a person who had been sent to
Europe to acquire the art of instructing the deaf and who had
come back with a competent teacher, who was himself deaf. The
roles of Dr. T. H. Gallaudet and Laurent Clerc were thus revealed
to the promoters in New York. What is more, they had themselves come to New York to solicit contributions and subscrip-
tions on behalf of their institution. Taken by surprise, the New
York committee floundered momentarily. Moreover, it became
clear that there really was no one in the country who was capable of undertaking the education of the deaf and that it would
be advisable to wait to see how the Hartford school progressed,
and perhaps later to request that it supply teachers. Although
New York had rushed into activity, as a consequence of Gard's
letter, it was in absolute ignorance that a trial was already under
way in Hartford. They recognized that they should do nothing
to delay or impede its progress. As it turned out, New York even
sent some pupils to the Hartford school.

But the promoters had not abandoned their objectives. They
simply waited until public opinion was better informed. Surveys
were undertaken. They concluded that if the ratio of the deaf in

the state as a whole was similar to that in New York City, there would be from 400 to 500 children in need of instruction. One school would not be sufficient for this number. They also became aware of the disadvantages and obstacles to sending children outside the state for such education. In short, they kept on with their task and in the spring of 1817, a list of administrators and trustees was drawn up, at the head of which was the name of De Witt Clinton, who later became governor of the state of New York, but stayed on the board. The organizing committee obtained an Act of Incorporation from the state legislature on 15 April, 1817. The institution then existed legally but only on paper.

In most cases, schools for the deaf sprang up at random and on their own. They then received recognition if they gave proof of successful operation. Here, the institution was conceptualized long before it became a reality. But to assure its full success, the assent and cooperation of the government were obtained in advance. This proved to be a very astute move.

It took the planners almost a year to organize their institution, furnish their buildings, appoint administrators, and obtain funding. The school formally opened in May 1818. Thus, Hartford must be counted as the first American school for the deaf, with an advance of one year. But the New York school can boast of being the first and the oldest school employing the oral method. One of the first acts of the trustees was to requisition a teacher from England. The committee was convinced that the speech method introduced by Braidwood was of greater value than the French system of de l'Épée, which was rejected. But Joseph Watson, the nephew of the famous Braidwood, was able only to send his syllabus. This booklet served the New York school as a guide. By way of comparison, the French school at Asnières followed exactly the same procedure, relying on the course in speech and lipreading prepared by Ludovic Goguillot.

In conclusion, Mr. Currier stressed the fact that the real founder of the New York Institution was the Rev. John Stanford of whom he spoke most eloquently. He observed that Stanford believed firmly, loved fervently, prayed ardently, walked humbly, worked diligently, waited patiently, and died triumphantly, for God was with him. Mr. Currier concluded by reaffirming that the institution would continue to make the deaf into productive citizens of a great state that had recognized its responsibilities on such an expansive and liberal scale. This is the best praise for its activity and for the government that was so supportive of its foundation.

When we think of F. Gard, it is hard not to feel some sadness. Gallaudet had visited him in Bordeaux two years earlier and had offered to take him back with him to America. But since Gard held to his original demands, Gallaudet went back to Paris and convinced Laurent Clerc to accompany him instead. Then Gard, who like his counterpart Clerc certainly wished to be the apostle to the deaf of the New World, for otherwise he would not have learned English as he did, tried to exert some influence on the consul Lee in order to find him a position in New York. But, unfortunately, New Yorkers' preference for the oral method scotched his dreams.

We were invited to have lunch with Mr. Hodgson at the teachers' table. We found a large attractive dining hall and a sea of white tablecloths. All the teachers and instructors have their meals at the institution, with the exception of those who live in the city. In view of the holidays, only a few places were occupied by members of the staff in charge of supervising the pupils whose parents had been unable to take them home for the summer.

As is the American custom, lunch was a light meal, more like an English tea, with cold cuts of meat and fruit. And, indeed, some excellent tea was offered as a drink.

The institution's food services were a world of their own. Our visit to the basement,where the kitchens are located, along with the bakery and its fiery ovens, the pantries with their cans and boxes, the laundry, astonished us. Everything is laid out according to a linear plan, grouped by specialties. Here there are giant vats for soup, there, grills for meat, in another part, the kitchen for the teachers. Dumb waiters carry the dishes up to the dining halls. There are machines for slicing bread, meat, and for other unknown operations. Numerous employees, men and women, white and black, are busy in the cellars where instead of casks and bottles of wine there are only ice-making machines.

Another source of amazement is the laundry. It was huge, filled with rumbling machines and hardworking women, even though the school was nearly empty. Almost all the laundry is machine-washed and rinsed. The clothing is strung on frames that are moved into heated rooms where it quickly dries. The napkins, handkerchiefs, towels, etc. are ironed and folded mechanically. For other items such as shirts, blouses, aprons, etc., the industrious women iron them by hand. As the school values neatness and white is the preferred color, this is a continuous task. The operating expenses of the laundry amount to $4,000 per year.

Next to the laundry is the power plant that is responsible for heating and lighting. We saw the powerful generators but the stifling heat prevented us from staying long.

Another building that we saw from a distance, with three or four stories, was the infirmary for infectious diseases.

We passed through the long, wide dining hall for the pupils. In the distance, we saw a group of girls with their supervisor who were playing or talking; friendly, alert faces. Then some lads, very correct in their uniforms, passed us with intelligent expressions on their faces. They gladly came over to speak to us and showed us the musical instruments that were kept in glass cases along the walls. They explained to us how they arranged to keep in time. They told us that they were almost all good bandsmen and spoke of having been reviewed by regular Army officers and of the congratulations that they had received. These young cadets made a very favorable impression on us and we were sorry not to have seen them drilling.

By way of an underground corridor, which protected us from a sudden shower, we made our way to the workshop. It was generously proportioned and stood in the center of a large open field, surrounded by asphalt pavement, very much like a parade ground. Here the cadets carried out their drills.

A tout seigneur tout honneur. To every man his due. We went up to the second floor where we found, wide and long with high walls and filled with light, the composing and printing shop run by Mr. Hodgson, who was assisted by Mr. Anthony Capelli, one of his former pupils.

There were a dozen apprentices in front of the compositors' trays, those who were spending their holidays at the school or who decided to stay on in order to earn a bit of money before classes resumed or they were placed with some private company. Arrangements like this assured the regular appearance of *The Deaf-Mutes' Journal* despite the fact classes had been suspended.

For this wonderful newspaper for the American deaf is printed right here. And this is no small undertaking, it is of the same size as a Paris daily: seven long pages with seven columns each of compact type. Since it is published once a week, every Thursday, the apprentices have to work rapidly with typesetting so that the paper is made up by Wednesday and can be passed at once to the presses. Their printing press is modern, rapid, and goodlooking, electrically powered. They have a second press for smaller jobs.

Here too they print the institution's reports, wonderful products of the typographer's art, and other works, some of which are commissioned by outside agencies, and some by other organizations of the deaf.

It is not just rote composing that the apprentices learn, line by line, as is the case on the rue St. Jacques in Paris. They learn all about commercial printing as well, invitations, advertisements, announcements, flyers, invoices, catalogs, business cards, programs. Here there was a rich collection of fonts and rules, some very artistic. Both classic American and the latest imaginative typefaces were represented. Mr. Hodgson is a very skilled typographer. All the apprentices that he trains find good positions without difficulty and earn good wages. We cannot say so much for those who graduate from the typesetting program at the Paris institution, despite the good will of the administration and the rigorous criticism of competent people, among whom the former Paris deputy Allemand, himself once a typesetter.

But Mr. Hodgson is also an accomplished writer, in both prose and verse, and a fine journalist, with a nose for news, extensive knowledge of the deaf community and of the means to further their social advance. He has taken a major role in all congresses of the deaf. He attended our congresses in Paris in 1889 and 1912 and his participation was greatly appreciated.

He became deaf at a rather advanced age, sixteen I believe, and continues to express himself in speech. He often gives public addresses, as was the case at the special commemorative session in Hartford at which he presented orally the masterly report of which we have reproduced portions. We are told that his voice is well understood, distinct, and still well modulated. He is, then, one of the most engaged of the deaf activists and has shown great initiative and perseverance in our emancipation.

He is also a great friend of France, knows our language, and has translated numerous articles. He was the linchpin for the fundraising campaign for deaf French flood victims in 1910 and for deaf French and Belgian victims of the invasion of 1913. We would also have liked to have reported on Dr. Thomas Francis Fox, another distinguished deaf teacher at the school, and also its librarian, but he was unfortunately absent, having just remarried.

Our visit went on for some time. We asked questions of the pupils, we interrogated their teacher who kindly gave us all the information we sought. Among the other samples of his apprentices' work, he gave us a bound collection of back issues of a tiny newspaper, the size of a playing card and entitled *The Little Printer,* which is intended for the pupils and keeps them up to date on the news of the institution.

On the walls are photographs of the groups, societies, and congresses in which Mr. Hodgson has taken part. We had the pleasure to note there photographs from our meetings in Paris and Versailles. All this was not without interest for the pupils and showed them what their older brothers were capable of through their collective spirit, solidarity, fraternity, accompanied by intelligence and hard work.

The Deaf-Mutes' Journal, which they typeset and print, is also a profitable form of teaching. Working on it, they not only get an idea of what civic life beyond the school is like, but their sense of competition is also stimulated, readying them for their eventual entry into a rough-and-tumble world.

In addition, it is a real windfall that the principal organ for advancing the cause of the American deaf can be printed at a reasonable price at the Washington Heights Institution. The higher printing costs that they would meet in the city would probably prove an obstacle to the regular appearance of the paper, as happens to other independent publications, with perhaps the exception of that published by the Frats. By supporting *The Deaf-Mutes' Journal*, the New York Institution renders an important new service to the general cause of the deaf.

The League of Elect Surds

On Saturday, July 14, in the afternoon, we were invited to an outing of the League of Elect Surds that was to take place in Ulmer Park, on the other side of Brooklyn and not that far from Coney Island.

Samuel Frankenheimer was kind enough to offer to get us there, for the spot was not easy to find, at least for those going there for the first time. We had to change trains at Brooklyn Bridge, the famous metal bridge that separates the two cities, and then once again a bit farther on.

As in England, Saturday afternoon off from work is scrupulously observed in the United States. I had already noted this in 1893. Now this is catching on in France, a social necessity that is imposing itself. In the course of our trip we saw how beneficial it was to the deaf community.

The social life of the deaf, like that of the hearing, occurs on Saturdays. Religious observances and family life take up Sundays, which is also as rigorously observed as in England. The bars and cafés are closed.

It is then on Saturday that the various organizations hold their events in turn. Sometimes there are two at the same time, not from any desire to compete but because circumstances make it impossible to do otherwise. But, generally, there is a good understanding among deaf organizations in scheduling events.

The League of Elect Surds was already in existence in 1893 during my first trip. On the elegant program that we were given as we entered we found our names and those of four French colleagues among the honorary members: Henri Gaillard, Joseph Chazal, R. V. Desperriers, Henry Genis, Fernand Hamar, Felix Plessis, Emile Mercier, and Henri Mercier, all of whom had received this honor when they visited the club. This time they had neglected, perhaps inadvertently, to add the names of Edmond Pilet, Eugène Graff, and Jean Olivier. But it would have been difficult to remember to do so because this was no formal meeting of the group. We were outdoors, at a spot erroneously called a park, for there were scarcely any trees, just a grassy track with a grandstand in front. On the track they played games and held races, even for ladies. There was also a large dance hall with a piano and a buffet. We had to pay to get in. In charge of arrangements were S. Kahn, A. Capelli, and H. C. Kohlman. There were about three hundred deaf people there, many of them extremely well dressed and attractive. Young people were in the majority. We were the objects of friendly curiosity.

There was a baseball game going on between two deaf athletic clubs, the Union League and the Men's Club of St. Ann of the Deaf. The objectives of the League of Elect Surds are to contribute to the well-being of its members and to the deaf in general, and in particular to raise the moral level of its members; to cultivate feelings of friendship among them; to assist those who might be in need as well as their families; to create ties among them; and to create an organization within which each can act for the common good.

Its motto is "Faith and confidence in God everywhere. Good will and love to all our brothers."

In the opinion of some of the deaf community, the League is modeled on a Masonic lodge. There is an initiation rite to enter. The administration consists of a grand ruler, Mr. Max Miller, a grand secretary, Charles J. Le Clerq, a grand treasurer, E. A. Hodgson, a grand tiler (doorkeeper), H. C. Kohlman, and so on.

The grand tiler was not much of a grand intercessor with the grand architect of the universe, for, toward evening a terrible storm broke out. Everyone took shelter in the dancehall, while lightning struck all around us and thunder rolled through our deafened ears with growling vibrations. We had never seen rainfall like that before in our lives. When it was time for us to leave to go the Frats banquet, the streets and roads had turned into lakes of water. We had to go along side streets in order to get to the streetcar.

The Banquet of Greater New York Division No. 23, National Fraternal Society of the Deaf

When we got off the street car, calm weather had returned. The rain was falling gently now and at Coney Island the lines of colored lights were coming on along the outlines of the buildings. We made our way to the Hollander restaurant which is a lot like a large Munich beerhall with countless tables in a courtyard, burdened with great drafts of beer, and with a band. It was here that Division No. 23, called the Greater New York Division, of the National Fraternal Society of the Deaf was giving a banquet in honor of the French delegation and the other American delegates to the Hartford Convention.

In a corner of the huge restaurant, two horseshoe-shaped sets of tables had been drawn up. This is how such fraternal banquets are preferentially held, almost on the same footing as for the other hearing customers, who displayed no indiscreet or offensive curiosity toward us.

It is the rule of the society that the members call each other "brother" and I was happy to conform. It was Brother Constantin, the secretary of the division, who served as toastmaster. He seated us at the table of honor, Graff and Olivier on one side, Pilet and me on the other, separated from the president by two eminent and charming oral deaf ladies, Mrs. Constantin and her sister, Miss Dorothy Norbitt, who was my companion.

Then we addressed ourselves to the dishes. The cooking was excellent, but what a thirst it caused! Even the national drink, ice water, was long in coming and we also had to wait for the fresh draft beer that we ordered at our own expense (seventy-five cents for a huge stein, please) despite our repeated orders. There were just not enough waiters.

Brother Constantin and Brother Pech, the past president of the division, began their speeches. Naturally, they praised the Frats, their brotherly objectives, their continuing progress. The speeches were received enthusiastically.

Mrs. Robert McVea signed the national anthem with fervor.

Then, the speeches followed in this order: Mr. Hodgson, Henri Gaillard, Nuboer, Pilet, Olivier, and the Rev. Keiser. The theme, from the French side, centered on congratulations for the wonderful work of mutual assistance accomplished by the Frats and our best wishes for its continued success.

To conclude, Mrs. Annie Lashbrook, gave us in signs the essential of another national song, "My Country 'tis of Thee."

It was past midnight when the dinner concluded. No one wanted to leave such an atmosphere of warm camaraderie. Outside, the fairyland of the spectacles drew us. But it was time to retire. First the elevated railroad with two transfers, then the streetcar to get us back to the hotel at three o'clock in the morning. Fortunately, in New York the subway and streetcars operate throughout the night.

ALBANY
On Advances Made by Deaf Americans

Visit to the High Commissioner of Education

Mr. Bailey took us to the Department of Public Education. There was a huge gallery running along the string of offices. Portable bulletin boards were set up at intervals, providing information and statistics on education in the state. Naturally, this prompted us to think of requesting information on the schools for the deaf. Mr. Bailey informed the office of the general secretary. A lady received us in respectful, friendly fashion. She referred us to another office where an employee took from various boxes a collection of reports and brochures on the eight institutions for the deaf that are under state supervision. We have spoken of these above.

Mr. Bailey returned to the general secretariat. He conversed with the distinguished-looking official in writing. The latter took up the telephone and our guide looked at us with an enigmatic smile. It was clear that he was setting something up. The lady listened and then made a gesture to wait. She took Mr. Bailey's notepad and asked him some questions about us. Suddenly, the phone rang, then the door opened and a young clerk came in. Mr. Bailey made a happy gesture and we all rose and bowed. We followed the young woman to the end of the corridor where she opened a door and were found ourselves in the presence of the high commissioner for education for the State of New York.

The room was huge, high-ceilinged and imposing; the furnishings were tasteful. But we did not have time to examine the paintings. The high commissioner came hurrying up from a corner cabinet. He put out his hands in a friendly way, had us be seated, and took a notepad in order to wish us welcome. But his face reminded me of something. It seemed that I had seen him somewhere before. Yes! It was on the steamship that brought us to America. The commissioner was among the first-class passengers, along with Dr. Carrel, and I believe that he had seen us in discussion. He had just come back from France. The eve of our departure from Bordeaux, I had in fact read in the *Petite Gironde* an article that gave an account of the enthusiastic welcome given at the University of Bordeaux to the Hon. John Huston Finley. It was he. We had no suspicion that he would be running the risk of submarines with us. And we could never have imagined that we would have the honor of being received by him, in whose jurisdiction the schools for the deaf lay.

Mr. John Huston Finley said that he had indeed seen us on the steamer. He gave us an account of his stay in France, his visits to all our universities, the high esteem in which he held French courage, the intellectual vigor of our professors and students. He admired the fact that almost all of them had made the sacrifice of their courage and youth for their country. Then he had us come into his office, and showed us the rich harvest of notes, books, brochures, and reports that he had accumulated on his journey. He did not want to be outdone by us, humble non-experts as we were. He made me a present of a bound book that gave an account of the memorable sessions during which he was invested as president of the University of New York. A photograph with strong lighting that resembled an engraving reproduced his energetic features, his studious and observant eye, and his friendly smile. As a dedication he wrote in: "In appreciation of the visit paid me by the honorable French delegation, John H. Finley, July 16, two days after July 14, 1917." Was not the homage rendered France via our humble representation deeply moving?

The elegant volume contained, among its many addresses, one from our ambassador, M. Jusserand. He was eager to convey the best wishes of France to Dr. Finley who was also a Chevalier de la Legion d'honneur. And M. Jusserand recalled that "in the cornerstone of many of the chief monuments of this country, a French amulet was placed and proved a good omen." Thus the State University of New York had been founded by two famous Americans, Alexander Hamilton and James Duane, in concert with a French Huguenot, L'Homedieu, who had come from La Rochelle, just like the ancestors of the Gallaudets.

In the same way, it was the French deaf-mute Laurent Clerc who assisted the descendants of the French Huguenots, the Gallaudets, to found the first school for the American deaf. And this confirms, as does so much else, the justifiable French pride of M. Jusserand.

We then took leave with the most cordial expression of good will of Mr. Finley.

Outside, we thanked and congratulated Mr. Bailey for having arranged such a fine surprise for us. M. Graff said that it gave evidence of the fine qualities of boldness and initiative that would stand him in good stead in advancing the social causes of the deaf.

Mr. Bailey then took us to the public library, which, like all the libraries of American cities, is a veritable palace with a majestic exterior and high classical colonnades. An elevator took us up to the reading room, which was filled with people buried in their books. The American people are always learning something new. Mr. Bailey asked one of the librarians to give us copies of the educational newspaper that was published for students, which had an account of the journey of the official French delegation with a fine photograph, crisp and smiling, of Marshal Joffre who is idolized by all the citizens of this vast country.

Outside, on the steps of the Capitol, a skilled deaf photographer, Milton Robertson, took some shots of our little group.

Dinner at the Round Table

We were expected at the Hampton Hotel at six o'clock in the evening. The most prominent deaf people in the community were giving a banquet in our honor. In a private room around a large round table, loaded down with bouquets of flowers, we took our seats. This is King Arthur's Round Table, one of our hosts fingerspelled.

The meal was plentiful, tasty and varied, doing honor to the kitchens of the Hampton Hotel and also to Mr. Bailey and his friends who in organizing the menu were eager, he said, to make us forget the poorly executed banquet in Hartford. It was, naturally, American cooking. But it is often excellent. In the absence of a "special little bottle of wine," the maitre d' solicitously poured us water from a crystal pitcher and added small ice cubes to our glasses. But one of the guests also suggested that we might like some beer. In that fashion we enjoyed the food all the better. Whatever you say, the Frenchman at a table with all the gourmet dishes that would please a Lucullus, if he does not find the pert charm of wine, will find it a sad state of affairs. In this regard, I may perhaps be allowed to recall what I said to my charming companion at the banquet in Chicago in 1893, Miss Cora E. Coe: "Yes, Americans have made a great deal of progress. But if they drank wine, instead of that insipid water and the diluted alcohol of cocktails, they would make even more."

During dessert, everyone proposed a toast: Messrs. Bailey, Gaillard, Pilet, Graff, Olivier, and Morin. The toasts were moving, warm with gratitude toward us and full of fraternal American feeling for France. Our hosts, Arthur T. Bailey, Edward Klier, Joseph Cermack, Harold R. MacQuade, Milton A. Robertson, and Philip Morin, jointly offered us a small flag, or rather a silk scarf in the American colors.

The Conference

After the dinner we were taken to the Elks Club. This is an Irish-American secret society that had kindly loaned out its huge meeting hall to the deaf. The meeting had been organized by the Albany section of the National Fraternal Society of the Deaf, or the Frats. In all haste they had convoked everyone they could reach. When we arrived on the stage, the deaf men and women, some hundred in all, were seated on rows of chairs facing each other, the curious seating arrangements that are modeled on the British House of Commons. Only the chairman, that is, President Bailey, was on the stage with us, our other hosts also being seated in order of rank in a single row.

Mr. Bailey introduced us. An ovation of raised arms received us and increased in agitation. Mr. Bailey opened the meeting by singing *America the Beautiful* in rhythmical signs. Then Mr. Frank E. W. MacMahon, of Troy, signed the *Marseillaise*. This was a revelation for us. His signing was ample and spirited and it progressed in time with his foot that soundly tapped the beat. The public had risen for the signing of the two national anthems. A tempest of applause followed Mr. MacMahon's performance.

Then, we gave our brief signed speeches in turn. Here, as elsewhere in the course of our journey, we said roughly the same things, with variations and longer and shorter treatment of specific topics on the reciprocal and century-long affection between the two countries; France's great appreciation for America's intervention in a war of justice; homage to President Wilson, to the Gallaudets, to the progress accomplished by Americans, and in particular to deaf education; reflections on advances made by deaf Americans that the French had reason to envy; on the certainty of victory; on the hope, after the war, of working together in closer fashion to improve the lot of the deaf of the entire world.

M. Pilet emphasized mutual assistance programs, M. Graff deaf organizations and clubs. M. Olivier particularly engaged the interest of the public with his account of the capture of the city of Rheims by the Germans, its recapture by the French army after the battle of the Marne, his long stay in the city under siege, the bombing of the cathedral, and the destruction of the city. He had the secret of kindling the anger of his deaf public, to such a point that Mr. MacMahon, who had returned to the stage, undertook with energetic, irritated, and vengeful signs a denunciation of German barbarity as no other deaf person could have done it. He was answered with unanimous applause.

Mr. Morin, the vice president, explained everything that Americans owed to France, in particular from the point of view of the education of the deaf. "Bravos!" showed to what extent he reflected the sentiments of those present.

Philip Morin had a very French name. He said that he was from Canada. He had been in Hartford where his cordiality and concern for our well-being had made a very positive impression on us.

Again Mr. MacMahon returned to the rostrum. This time it was in order to sign in more conventional but deeply stirring fashion the poem "The Ancient Oak" about the eve of Waterloo by the great American poet Bryant. We expressed our admiration. At the end, the public rose to exclaim with their hands "Vive la France!" "Long live France!" to which we replied by fingerspelling "Vive l'Amérique!"

Mr. Bailey came forward to present us with a pair of American flags that had been decorating the stage. We took the neighboring French flags and presented them to him in turn, asking him to keep them in memory of our visit. Then, Gaillard unfolded the American scarf that he had been given, kissed it with passion, and waved it amidst the general enthusiasm. With that, the meeting closed.

We went down to one of the rooms in the basement. A reception had been organized, with ice cream and glasses of water.

The deaf ladies were extremely charming to us. But the Elks had gotten wind of our presence. In a large neighboring room, a number of them were seated at tables. Mr. Bailey introduced us. By way of thanks for the hospitality that had been shown the French and American deaf, we presented them with two French flags. They were moved by this gesture and gave an order that the French tricolor should have a place of honor over a large monumental fireplace. Then they invited us into the private bar. We toasted each other with an extra-strong Irish gin that is cut with half a glass of Bordeaux and that has to be downed in a single drink and then followed by a glass of ice water. It burned our chests but the water put out the fire in our innards. This was a rather brutal gustatory experience! The fumes rose to our heads. A matter of taste or of habit, I suppose. But the second round that was offered made us wary and, instead, well drawn drafts of tasty, fresh beer made us forget the puritanical water that accompanied the ice cream.

On our notepads, writing in English, these Irishmen expressed the regard and admiration they had for France and their anger against the autocratic German invader who threatened world peace.

It was late in the evening when we said goodnight to our hosts. With a great show of feeling we thanked Messrs. Bailey, Morin, Robertson, and the representatives of the Frats, who had covered all our expenses down to the last dime.

The next morning, our hosts had all returned to work. They had only requested one day off in order to receive us. Around noon of that same day we left by train for Buffalo.

BUFFALO
A Charming and Friendly Welcome

The Roman Catholic Institution
of Le Couteulx Sainte-Marie

As we sat in the long railway car, wide and bright, with rows of seats for two passengers on each side of the aisle and tables that went up and down, we saw some young men who were signing. One of them greeted us, saying that he had seen us at a picnic in Ulmer Park. He informed us that they were on their way to look for work in Akron, some out of curiosity, the desire for a change, and to see something of the country, others because unemployment was rising in the fashionable industries of New York. There were eight of them, well dressed, intelligent and determined. We talked quite a lot during the long trip, but we could not be gone long from our seats, since new passengers were getting on at every station.

One of these, in fact, came in and took M. Olivier's seat, when he had gone to smoke his pipe in the smoker. When our colleague returned, the other passenger apologized in English. With a quick gesture, M. Olivier made him understand that he did not hear. Then the other man at once began to fingerspell, in English, naturally. As I was seated behind them, I intervened.

When he learned that we were French, our new companion was extremely pleased. He gave us his business card. Mr. Cary, from Elmira, near New York. He said that he was of French descent on his mother's side and that he had learned the manual alphabet at college. He showed us some medical radiography plates that he had in a leather case. It turned out that he was a surgeon and was going to Buffalo to operate. We were on our way to Niagara Falls but were obliged to stay overnight in Buffalo which we would reach in the evening. The eight young deaf men, on the other hand, would change trains there for Cleveland.

I had been given a number of useful addresses in Buffalo. But I had not counted on us having the time to stay there very long. Still, I was very interested in visiting a Roman Catholic institution for the deaf that is among the most remarkable and perhaps the most important in the New World. Ignorant of how much time we would have at our disposal, I had hesitated to alert the Superior, the Rev. Mother Mary Anne Burke. Now, as it happened, the train brought us into Buffalo right at six in the late afternoon and it was still broad daylight. If we took a streetcar, perhaps we might still have time to try to see the school.

I asked Mr. Cary for his advice. In his opinion it seemed quite possible and he offered to accompany us. But, first, he wanted to take us to a restaurant and get us a room because most of the hotels were full up. When we were finally free to leave, it was already dark and we thought that there was no longer any way at such an hour of going and knocking on the door of a school, especially one run by nuns. Mr. Cary reassured us. However, we lost even more time waiting at a streetcar stop where we had to transfer. This was all the more striking because Buffalo was the place where these switching plates were invented and in Paris they are called *buffalos*. And it took a rather long time for the streetcar to take us there, which was proof that the institution was located well outside the city, although still on its main street.

The street numbers were up in the 2250s by the time we arrived. And the street kept on going. Trees, lawns, private homes, big buildings.

In the half-light of evening, the electric streetlights projected wavering light into corners of darkness beyond their regular reach and we finally found the school. The wicker gate was open. We crossed a driveway cutting through an immense lawn and went up a handsome flight of steps. Mr. Cary rang the bell. A nun appeared. At a word from our guide and without the least hesitation, the door was opened wide. There were gas lights on the walls and it was nearly nine o'clock in the evening.

Foreign visitors who might have appeared in a hurry at one of our French schools under similar circumstances would have been turned away without the least expression of courtesy.

We presented our apologies. But with clear and graceful signs, the good sister said how pleased she was to receive us. But she regretted to inform us that the Mother Superior was absent. She expressed a wish that we might be able to return the next day to see her.

She had us sign the visitors' book.

We went up a short stairway reserved for visitors which opened onto a reception room. Some nuns were gathered there and others soon arrived. We were given a friendly and charming welcome. All of them, even the youngest, used sign language with the clarity and grace proper to their sex. What a pleasure it was for us! And what a difference from the nuns in Bordeaux, the youngest of whom refused to employ sign language. The older ones, who knew how to sign, would scarcely consent to do so in public except to chat with their former pupils who had lost the habit of speaking. In Buffalo, however, the oral method was in use and, as we shall see in a moment, better was still to come. The school administration had understood that the best way for a teacher of the deaf to know all the secrets of his or her art and to grasp the complex and varied mentality of the pupils was to know the natural and habitual language of signs as well as newer pedagogical methods. This used to be a requirement for admission into the national teacher training program in Paris. We would do well to return to those days. Young oralist teachers would be informed of the pedagogical value of signing and

[handwritten margin note, right side: Nuns in Bordeaux → Youngen—required to sign. oldem—knew but required to sign in public]

*[handwritten note, bottom: *Military training for boys is no longer done. More manual labor, less as education]*

they would in addition have a means of communication with the adult deaf who had been exposed to the oral method to a greater or lesser degree. We would then never again have to witness the sorry spectacle of teachers called as interpreters for the deaf before the courts of law who stated, to the astonishment of the judges, that they didn't even know how to finger spell.

Some pupils had stayed at the school over the summer holidays and they were introduced to us. They were lively, resourceful, and polite. They showed us their handiwork which was on exhibit in the room after the most recent award of prizes. There were embroideries, baptismal gowns, religious miniatures, dainty women's crafts, small religious objects. We saw that they had nimble fingers and good taste.

One of the deaf instructors from the typographical workshop, Mr. Walter W. Wheeldon, whom we had seen in Hartford, came to shake our hands. He brought us the institutional newspaper, *The Le Couteulx Leader*, which was printed there. In the upper left hand corner of the first page were the portraits of the Abbé de l'Épée, Abbé Sicard, and Father Timon. Below and to the right, the Star Spangled Banner and the Tricolor, joined by a branch of laurel. This made evident the French origins of the institution. It was, in fact, a wealthy American of French extraction, as his name Le Couteulx indicates, who provided the means to establish the institution about sixty years ago. A huge oil painting, hung in one of the reception rooms, presented the distinguished and kindly face of this prominent city resident of an earlier era. And his name inscribed atop the building also perpetuated his memory among the grateful deaf and their friends.

Sister Mary Emerentia, who ran the printing shop, reported on the school's activities from September 30, 1912, to September 30, 1914. What particularly distinguished the booklet was the quality of the photoengravings which, according to Napoleon's famous precept, "the simplest sketch tells me more than a long report," gave clear proof of the well-run classes, the industry of the teachers and pupils in mixed classes (at least in instructional settings), and the level of material comfort at the institution.

The school, as noted, is operated under the auspices of the Roman Catholic Church and takes in deaf and mute children of that faith. It is administered by a board of trustees whose chairman was the Hon. George A. Lewis, with the Rev. Colton as vice-chairman and Rev. Gilmore as secretary. The last-named is also known for his sermons to the deaf. Sister M. Alesius is the superintendent and Sister Mary Anne Burke the principal. Sister M. Constantia is the vice principal. A lay person, Miss Julia M. Connery, is in charge of oral instruction.

The teaching staff consists of some twenty nuns and other lay women. Rather few trades are taught at the school: painting and draftsmanship, typesetting and tailoring for boys; dressmaking, sewing, home economics for girls. But I am sure that the pupils, once they had completed their basic education, would be in a position to take up other vocations after leaving school, if they so chose.

The number of pupils varies between 160 and 180. About eighty were receiving support from the State of New York. Another seventy came from neighboring states; only ten pupils had their costs fully borne by their families.

Fundamentally, instruction is based on the pure oral method. Indeed, it was with this objective in mind that the nuns engaged Miss Connery, who had earlier taught for sixteen years on Lexington Avenue in New York. Miss Connery is very skilled in applying the latest advances in the art (or science) of speech, according to the Miller method. She pays particular attention to rhythmical exercises to assist in the production of speech with the help of vibrations from a piano on which the pupils place their hands. In this way they perceive the various sonorities and this, it would seem, gives them a better sense of harmony. Their articulation improves and lipreading also becomes easier.

Since classes had been suspended for the summer holidays, it was not possible for us to judge the quality of the results obtained with the new method. But the pupils who were still in residence showed us clearly that they spoke, read lips, but also signed. We concluded that the combined method had not been entirely banned from the Buffalo institution, which had earlier long championed it.

In addition to physical education under the direction of Miss Leonard, the boys received military training from Corporal A. Follett, under the direction of Captain Gillig of the 74th Regiment of the New York State National Guard.

Sister M. Euphemia, who was in charge of the painting workshop, took us into her domain. It was a huge studio filled with canvases on easels, framed paintings and engravings hung on the walls, statuettes—all the work of the pupils. There were some very fine pieces there.

Up stairs, along passageways and corridors, we were shown around the other parts of the building. The dining halls were a far cry from those that we were accustomed to see in France. Chairs and tables with tablecloths, plates, elegant cutlery and sets of glass salt and pepper shakers. From this you can judge the level of the remainder, the dormitories, bathrooms, classrooms, and so on.

Sister Emerentia and Mr. Wheeldon showed us the printing shop. It had just been moved to a newly constructed building that had been specially designed for industrial training. The printing shop was vast, with several rows of compositors' trays and two treadles for printing. Not only do they print the *Leader* and various reports, they also do commercial work. Invitations, announcements, brochures for the city and for business are produced according to the highest standards for the school's clients who appreciate the skill of the young deaf trainees.

In another building what we particularly admired was the heating plant, the generators, ice-making machines, the bakery, laundryroom. All of this made up an imposing physical plant that assured the school's lighting, heating, cool air, cleanliness, and ease of operation, in short its superior level of material comfort.

It was clear that this Catholic institution was in the lead of deaf education in America.

We congratulated and thanked the dedicated nuns who were responsible for this achievement.

The institution in Buffalo, a city called the Queen of the Lakes, proves that religion, when it joins science to devotion and shows a concern for the dignity of man and woman with not only heaven in mind but also life here on earth, can be of true value for humanity.

For more than a half century and still today, Mother Mary Anne Burke has had but a single thought, to advance the cause of the institution. She deserves the greatest praise. On the occasion of her vocational anniversary former pupils gave her striking proof of their gratitude.

AKRON
Mecca of Opportunity

A Worker Community of 350 Deaf

The trip by train along the Ohio River, its water colored yellow by the clay, was interesting. Rich fields and market gardens, fields of grain, vines and orchards; towns and villages, some of which have French names; views of Lake Erie in the distance; and, toward noon Western Time, one hour behind New York, the rapid and comfortable train of the Ohio Railroad brought us to Cleveland, a large city in the state of Ohio.

We had to get off in order to take a branch line to Akron.

At the information window we learned that we had an almost three-hour wait ahead of us before the departure. We went to Parcels, a very convenient American invention, and left our hand baggage. Then, we set off into the city by streetcar.

Wide streets, monumental squares, lavish building fronts, far too many temperance restaurants, hurried passers-by on the side-walks, streetcars and speedy cars on the pavement, these charac-terized Cleveland as they do all American cities.

We succeeded in locating a restaurant that served beer that looked a bit like a German beer hall, but whose manager was simply called Gobert, which is a very French name. We ate and slaked our thirst in comfort. The heat was oppressive, and we sensed a storm behind the gray cloud cover.

Through the restaurant window we could make out a branch office of the Goodyear Tire and Rubber Company. Although we had already telegraphed Mr. Ashland Martin of our arrival, we went in to inquire whether it was possible to get to the factory by some other means than the railroad. A telephone call was placed and we were informed that we could save an hour by taking a one-hour streetcar ride. Better this than wasting our time wandering around without a fixed goal.

The electrified streetcar, huge and powerful, crossed the outlying areas of the city, made up of dark, smoke-stained houses in the shadow of the giant chimneys of the factories. Then, we were out in the country, passing through delightful fields, along graceful avenues of trees—a charming landscape. Suddenly, there was a great surge of wind and the storm broke out, quickly and violently. A torrential downpour whipped the car, which like an artillery shell pursued its trajectory unperturbed. We felt like we were seated within the shelter of a glass case, projected through the furious outbreak of a tempest. Finally, after twenty minutes, the storm died down. We raised the windows and a fresh and pleasant smell rose from the greenery. The ozone in the air revivified us.

We wondered whether we would ever reach Akron. The track stretched on, bright in the returning sunlight. Then, cottages and bungalows began to appear along the way. What a surprise! We thought Akron was only a little town like any other, and this row of houses pointed to a considerable community. Soon the streetcar stopped at an intersection, in the middle of an inextricable mixture of vehicles and a swarming crowd of people. We felt suddenly disoriented. And we remembered that we had agreed to meet Mr. Ashland Martin at the railroad station.

People told us to take another streetcar that passed by the Goodyear factory. The conductor promised to point it out to us.

*racial issues → foreigners worked in great labor conditions, want dealt in good, like white Americans.

Then, after a long ride, we spotted people signing, leaning on their elbows or sitting on the railing of a bridge, then others coming and going, or standing around. A whole population of deaf! We got off the streetcar in front of the management building. The doorman telephoned up to the offices. An employee came down and explained to us that Mr. Martin had left. Since he had brothers in the army in France, he was eager to receive us and give evidence of his support for France. We set out to look for Mr. Martin. The first group of deaf that we came up to told us that he had left for the station by automobile. Darn! What a pity to have troubled him needlessly! But we were led to a group of deaf in a café. One of them jumped on a bicycle and sped off to the station to inform Mr. Martin of our arrival. We, however, were taken back to the factory management building. On the way, we and the Akron deaf asked each other all sorts of questions. We met two groups of deaf people coming from the opposite direction. They were hesitant to come up to us, given our unaccustomed appearance and the large crowd around us. I caught one of them, with a humorous expression, ironically fingerspelling "spies." The others were incredulous. "What, spies?" But I turned back and signed, "You can laugh if you want but we are French." The other fellow laughed too, because someone who had been in the train with us from Buffalo had protested. We shook hands all around, bowing and signing greetings. Suddenly, an automobile stopped at the edge of the sidewalk. In the driver's seat we recognized deaf Mr. Faucher who had driven us around Hartford. Mr. Ashland D. Martin jumped from the auto with his hands outstretched. We offered our apologies for having deviated from the arrival plans in order to come and leave a bit earlier. "But, not at all," he said, "You are of course excused, and will be our guests this evening, and tomorrow as well if you can. Besides, you will have to have two get-togethers: one this evening for those who will be working tomorrow, and another tomorrow morning for people working tonight." So much graciousness and understanding of the pur-

Firestone, like Goodyear, employed many deaf workers

pose of our trip, to promote support for France, that we were easily convinced to accept his offer.

Mr. Faucher invited us to come and dine at a family-run restaurant and boarding house where a number of deaf came to eat. The meal was simple and substantial, and gave us a glimpse into the ordinary diet of American workers: bread and butter, boiled potatoes, green beans, beef, roast veal, a lettuce and tomato salad, jam, cherries, cheese, pies, water, and coffee. There were innumerable boarding houses like this that offered rooms and meals. Almost all the deaf in Akron lived in places like this, except for those very few who were married and had their own homes.

It would seem that many were there only to earn money and then went off back to their home communities when they had saved up a nest egg. Hearing workers did the same. Any ordinary factory worker who stayed eight years on the same job got his picture published in the newspaper of the company, or rather of the Clan of Goodyearites, for the paper was called *The Wingfoot Clan*, the winged foot, symbol of speed, being the company emblem.

There were, however, at least two deaf men who had been there for twenty-five years.

We were introduced to deaf people come from all the states of the Union, Germans and Austrians, naturalized Italians, even a Belgian, who addressed us in proper French.

We were astonished to learn of two deaf teachers who had come from distant schools. They admitted that they were there only for the summer holidays in order to earn the good extra money, since they were so poorly paid where they lived and worked.

Akron is called the *Mecca of Opportunity*, because anyone who comes there can find employment and earn well.

The salaries appeared high to us. Almost everyone told us that they earned between three and six dollars a day. But we lacked information to determine whether the cost of living permitted them to save any of this money. A letter that had been published said that there was no truth in this claim of a Mecca, that the salaries were an illusion, and that those who came to Akron were skinned by the local storekeepers. The writer was perhaps some deaf malcontent who didn't know how to handle his affairs. Since everyone who talked to us said that they were happy in their work, that they were well paid, and were making substantial savings, we were inclined to believe them.

But the important fact, which is remarkable from the sociological point of view, is that somewhere in the world there is a large industrial company that has not scorned deaf workers, has even sought them out, but with no aim of exploiting them, and pays them on the same scale as hearing workers. Equal pay for equal work. At first and hesitantly, the company hired only a dozen deaf workers. By the month of March, there were more than a hundred. And when we visited the plant, there were 350, divided into three eight-hour shifts: night, day, and afternoon shifts. (At the time of this writing, their number has grown to more than 500.)

The Goodyear Tire and Rubber Company manufactures rubber products. The rubber arrives raw. It is refined, processed, and leaves the factory as a thousand different products, but principally in the form of pneumatic tires for carriages, bicycles, and above all automobiles. Labor was intense on this last product line, because the factory had been requisitioned by the Secretary of State for the war effort. For this reason, detectives guarded the entry to the plant and suspiciously examined the visitors' passes that Mr. Martin had issued to us. And, inside, the foremen in all the shops would ask to see and check them.

It was on the ground and basement floors that the power-driven manufacturing operations were carried out, and it was here that the deaf were employed. Do not expect me to give a description of this huge factory that employs 20,000 workers. Our visit was too superficial and short. And we lack the technical knowledge. But we recognized that the work was specialized, in order to produce without delay and under strictly controlled conditions a range of finished and fault-free products. This involved various manufacturing departments. In some of these departments we met deaf men working in teams of twelve to fifteen with hearing comrades. Some laid out the strips of rubber, others rounded off the edges that would face the wheel rims. One group fused the rubber into hard, solid tires; another finished them off, ready to be sent to the factory stores.

Thus, from one section to another we ran into teams of deaf workers. We found some working with trowels, others engaged in curing the tires by baking them in sealed furnaces where any human being would be asphyxiated and horribly burned in the space of a second. In fact, the heat was stifling in the whole hall.

All the deaf workers expressed their delight at shaking hands with deaf Frenchmen, and they thanked us for our visit and wished us well. They signed their admiration for General Joffre and the French army, their anger at Germany, which had destroyed world peace, and their hope that American soldiers would help the French to punish Germany. About their work, they said that it was not so hard and they did not complain about their foremen. In fact, there were two deaf foremen and a third was the son of deaf parents and so was able to sign. But we couldn't chat away in sign language for too long. Like the hearing workers, each of the deaf had to apply himself and do the work expected of him for his wages. And since the work lasts eight hours a day, there was time enough to do a loyal day's work.

Relations with the hearing were marked by the most open fellowship. There was a true spirit of mutual assistance, we were told, among all the Goodyearites.

Seeing the huge number of conveyor belts, the revolving wheels of the machinery, even though they were surrounded by safety arrangements, we were anxious to learn whether the deaf had accidents. Hardly ever, we were told. They were naturally prudent. Things may happen to the careless. But a true accident was a rare, chance event, and he who suffered it was a victim of fate, like the pedestrian who slips on an orange peel on the sidewalk.

Accident statistics for the plant during the month of June, as published in *The Wingfoot Clan*, showed a total of 139 accidents for the 18,992 employees, or 7.3 per thousand workers. The great majority of these resulted from negligence. True accidents totaled only eighteen, which bore out the information I had for the deaf. Still, we would have liked to know how many of these might be injured in any year and in what ratio to the hearing.

We went down to other basement floors. The heat became denser, more oppressive. The atmosphere in Hell must be healthier! The most unhealthy and heavy work with the rubber was carried out in these underground shops, especially the baking. The raw rubber was melted in great vats and came out as rubber paste. This was the Goodyear technique.

In these departments there were no deaf workers. In fact, there were no American citizens. Only foreigners, immigrants—Poles, Slovaks, Ruthenians, Russians, Italians, Spaniards, and even Austrians—were willing to work at these terrible tasks. Yet among them, Germans seemed to be privileged. They did not work in the torrid, polluted atmosphere where the workmen breathed and swallowed the fibrous fumes. They stood in cold, glacial air, washing tires in huge tubs of cold water. Tall and

strong, their upper bodies and arms bare, just like the men who
worked at the hellish ovens, they curiously watched us pass.
How susceptible the workers must be to pneumonia or throat
infections, there where the temperatures were so exaggeratedly
disproportionate! One member of our delegation came down
with laryngitis and a cold that was later cured by the good graces
of a lady in Philadelphia.

Naturally, salaries were higher here than for normal work
categories. The men could make ten dollars a day. But there
were few who lasted. Illness or death was laying in wait for
them. As a result, almost all, when they had built up their savings, went looking for less dangerous work. But there was
always a way to replace them, despite the restrictive new immi-
gration laws.

Without doubt, the suffering proletariat was not being
attracted in the deceptive and mean ways described by Upton
Sinclair in his novel *The Jungle*. Here people were loyal and
straightforward. The high wages were the one honest promise.
As long as the exploitation of man by man continues, it will be
difficult to do otherwise, unless everyone were imposed a daily
hour of hard labor, which would perhaps be the Communist solu-
tion to the problem of necessary but onerous work. But I am
straying from my subject.

A freight elevator took us to the upper floors. Offices, stores.
Absolute solitude, complete calm. Everything was closed. There
was scarcely anyone on guard. A stairway. Long, wide corridors
between glassed-in offices. Classrooms. There was one for every
language. Mr. Ashland Martin turned an electrical switch. On the
frosted glass of a door the inscription informed us that was the
room for the "Mutes' Class." And Mr. Ashland Martin was in
charge. He was a teacher at the same time as being manager for
the deaf employees at the factory.

It was a real classroom with some twenty desks and school
benches. There were numerous similar classrooms along the
corridor. They were used by the foreign workers who did not
know English, who were instructed by teachers speaking the

language of the country from which they had immigrated. Naturally, French was not represented, because we scarcely send our sons abroad any more. As far as the deaf were concerned, who are here called *mutes* rather than *deaf*, which might have been a slur but was not, since they were all nativeborn Americans; this class served only to complement their prior education, improving their knowledge of English and upgrading their technical skills for the jobs they had. However, those of Russian and Polish-Jewish origin found material for study. The method was simple, and the books were elementary and clear. And Mr. Ashland Martin, from what we heard, was a patient and conscientious teacher. Not too much time had passed since he had left Gallaudet College where he obtained his degree. He was, then, still young. He had all the daring, all the studious and practical intelligence of vigorous and active youth. It was largely thanks to him and his untiring advocacy that the department of the deaf at the Goodyear plant had won so much ground.

But the gratitude of the deaf and of their friends in the United States, as in Europe and everywhere, should go to Mr. F. A. Seiberling, the chairman of the board of directors of the Goodyear Company; to Mr. Don Stevens, manager; Fred Fuller, assistant manager; G. B. Hodgkin, director of manufacturing operations; P. W. Workman, director of personnel. By admitting deaf workers, by favoring their employment, and in such considerable numbers, they have done humanity a great service. They have led a revolution against the prejudiced, ignorant and stupid, who believe that being deprived of the sense of hearing is enough to make you incapable of using your hands and your intelligence. To cite the telling phrase of a former French representative from the Department of the Seine, they rehabilitated the deaf in their own eyes. Better still, they showed their fellow-citizens that "mutes" are social resources that can be utilized even in the age of the machine, and that it is industrial nonsense, not to say a crime of homicide, to ban them from employment. This is, however, what is being done in certain plants and in many jurisdictions. And even those who have lost their hearing in the war find, more often than you may think, the door closed when they apply for vacant positions.

Moreover, in this industrial city of Akron, the other companies that competed with Goodyear, of which the most powerful employed 45,000 persons, steadfastly refused to employ the deaf.

It is then with extreme pleasure that I again congratulate the directors of the Goodyear Tire and Rubber Company for their lofty, positive, and enlightened spirit, and for their generosity, and I would cite their example to the heads of other companies that already employ deaf workers or who receive from them applications for work.

Leaving the factory, we headed for another building given over to management. We had requested a room for our presentation. But it was occupied and we had to wait for a bit. We profited by the free time to talk with each another, interrogating the Akron workers about their living and working conditions. The answers were unanimous. They liked it in Akron and they were well paid.

Finally, we were able to go up. A large reading room had been made available to us. Books and newspapers lay scattered on the tables. The Akron deaf did not yet have a club of their own. Perhaps they will have one in the future.

About one hundred deaf workers had gathered.

Mr. Ashland Martin introduced us. We were greeted with applause. And then we launched into our presentation, insisting particularly on the great social implications of what we had just seen, proving that in salaried work the deaf are worth just as much as the hearing. We added that surrounded by the generous fraternal hospitality accorded us by the deaf of Akron we did not regret our long voyage. In fact, our mission would not have fulfilled its mandate if we had failed to come and see for ourselves such a successful intensification in the social deployment of the deaf. We congratulated President Seiberling and the directors of Goodyear, and also Mr. Ashland Martin, who so worthily represented his comrades to management.

M. Jean Olivier concluded with what most interested the American deaf, an account of his experience in Rheims of the war. He made a vivid impression and received numerous expressions of sympathy.

We were then led to restore ourselves with some good fresh beer and copious sandwiches at a large bar where the factory workers crowded to the point of suffocation. Then, Mr. Faucher and Mr. Martin invited us for a tour of the city by automobile.

Mr. Faucher handled the steering wheel with mastery. He drove quickly and skillfully along the wide streets, which went off in the distance under a long line of electric lights, among factories with all their windows glowing like industrious beehives. The tour gave us an idea of the extent of Akron.

The Deaf Committee had offered to put us up at a clean and comfortable hotel, the ground floor of which also had at the same time a temperance bar, a tobacco and newspaper shop, and a novelty store. The next morning, after a proper breakfast with Mr. Martin and some others, it was to a church basement that we were taken. There, on Sundays, with the help of Mr. Martin and a hearing and speaking daughter of two deaf persons, Mrs. Mina Bard, religious services with signed sermons were offered the deaf population of Akron.

Mr. Bard, husband of the devoted and charming young woman just mentioned, was also the child of deaf parents and he was one of the overseers and interpreters for the deaf at the factory. We had seen him the previous day. Two other overseers were deaf, Mr. Heydey Bingham, a former student at the Mount Airy Institution in Philadelphia, and Alva Cowden, a former student of that in Columbus.

About one hundred deaf persons were still there, among whom were two ladies. We again made our presentation, this time somewhat amplified, and again we met the same sympathetic and fraternal reception.

On the way out, our photograph was taken under a blazing sun. Then Mr. Faucher's auto took us to the deaf workers' sports

Throughout his visit, Gaillard and the French delegation were able to observe and enjoy deaf social gatherings, as with the Lake Compounce outing in Connecticut and to the deaf sports field in Akron.

field which was adjacent to that of the hearing. Both were gifts of the factory owners.

The deaf sportsmen of Akron are famous. However, *The Wingfoot Clan* informed us that in the last competition the mutes had lost the first baseball game, which was a big surprise. But our comrades had their revenge the following Saturday.

There are several deaf associations in Akron: the savings club, a branch of the national association, another of the Fraternal Society (Division No. 55), and the Grace Mission, a branch of the Episcopalian Church of Saint Paul. At times the deaf minister, the Rev. Brewster R. Allabough, comes to preach. All these activities are subsidized and encouraged by the generosity of the directors of the Goodyear Tire and Rubber Company.

Toward eleven o'clock, Messrs. Ashland Martin and Faucher, and some others took us back to the car for Cleveland. We thanked them warmly for their gracious hospitality.

PITTSBURGH
With the Warmest Memories

Frank R. Gray

[handwritten marginalia: Politics: Civil service deaf dept → Out (mechanic's) Urbor, book binding, etc. to Taft opened civil service exams to deaf but no advanced degree.]

In order not to subject ourselves to the fatigue of a long train trip by night to Philadelphia, we decided to stop in Pittsburgh and spend a few evening hours there before sleeping at a hotel. It was also our intention to meet Frank R. Gray, a remarkable deaf man who knows French, has translated many of our articles and, in particular, has informed Americans about the celebrated inquest of Alfred Binet and Dr. Simon into the failure of the pure oral method.

We had forewarned Mr. Gray by telegram. But our train was almost a full hour late. So that when we arrived we searched in vain in the huge hall but found no one. We were on the point of leaving to get a hotel but decided to look one more time while signing among ourselves in order to attract attention. For my part, I looked closely at those who might resemble Mr. Gray, whose features I remembered from a photograph. Suddenly M. Pilet pointed out a gentleman who was walking slowly as if waiting for someone and whose bearded appearance was close to that which I recalled. I went up to him and we suddenly rec-

118

ognized each other, even though we had only seen each other's face in photographs.

Mr. Gray took us to one of the best hotels where an excellent meal was still available to us. And then we began to talk. Mr. Gray had graduated from Gallaudet College and had a master of science degree. He is perhaps the only deaf person in the whole world to be engaged in astronomy. He is employed by an agency that assures the quality control of optical instruments, telescopes, spectacles, lenses, and other objects of scientific investigation.

He is also a talented writer. He chairs the Pittsburgh Association of the Deaf. However, the state of his health no longer allows him to devote himself so generously to such activity. Yet he had wanted to do something to receive us, such as arranging a meeting with the city's deaf. At a minimum he would now take us to the association's premises in the hope that there might be some people present, even though Saturday evening was otherwise the favorite time to go there.

The Empty Club

A short stroll through the brilliantly lit streets, with skyscrapers rising into the night, brought us to a darker part of the city by a river that freshened us up a bit after the oppressive heat. Here was a large office building, rising two stories above a wide staircase, with glass doors, on one of which was printed "Society of Deaf-Mutes." Mr. Gray had a key and we entered. He pressed a button and electric light flowed over us, revealing two rooms, sufficiently spacious to serve the club's needs. In one was a billiard table, in the other, tables and chairs. On the walls were pictures, photographs of groups of deaf people, and a large blackboard on which Mr. Gray wrote: "The French delegates were here, but there was nobody home." I, in turn, wrote in English our greetings and fraternal best wishes. I still don't know what impression these lines may have made on the deaf of Pittsburgh. For his part, Mr. Gray, in *The Deaf-Mutes' Journal*, expressed his concern over what impression we might have had of his huge city, a gigantic worker community continuously engaged in the labors of the Cyclops. He can rest easy on that count. We had a good chance to look around. And we were deeply touched, in our French hearts, to see, as we made our way back to the hotel, groups of young people marching in the streets with American and French flags, in support of the war for liberty, while others, in front of the offices of a newspaper, dripping with electric lines, were impatiently waiting for the paper to learn whether they had been drafted, conscription being operated on a lottery basis. When we took the 7 a.m. express train for Philadelphia, Mr. Gray was there, despite his fatigue, to see us off. We thank him with the warmest memories.

PHILADELPHIA
For Our Little World

The Reception—Rev. Dantzer

I had already seen Philadelphia in 1893 and it was part of my plan to show my traveling companions the famous City of Brotherly Love, which is at the forefront of those cities with strong ties of affection to France.

And as luck would have it, the Rev. C. O. Dantzer, the deaf minister of the deaf Philadelphians, and Mrs. Syle, the deaf widow of the first American pastor, who founded the local deaf church, had been kind enough to give us an explicit invitation.

From Pittsburgh I sent Rev. Dantzer a telegram announcing our arrival. He was at the station to meet us and his welcome was brotherly and cordial. He then led us to the parcels office of a nearby local train station where we dropped off our hand baggage, and then to a very fashionable restaurant where he planned to have us taste Philadelphian cuisine. It was well prepared and tasty, although very spicy.

Rev. Dantzer informed us that but for the telegram he could very well have been absent. In fact, that Saturday afternoon the deaf citizens of the city had gone on a picnic to Atlantic City, on the shore, and his wife and Mrs. Syle were with them. They would not be getting home before midnight, as they were not expecting our visit. As for him, he had had to perform a wedding ceremony that morning, so that he was still in the city and able to get our telegram.

While waiting for the next train, we walked around the neighboring streets and he showed us the imposing historical buildings. He was like this during our whole stay in the city, for the Rev. Dantzer was an avid student of history and Philadelphia is rich in history and memorable landmarks. It was in the old town hall, since renamed Independence Hall, that the first congress was held, which proclaimed the liberty of the United States of America. We visited the building, and others as well. And in many spots they showed us places where George Washington had sat, and where he had prayed in church. We saluted the tomb of Franklin, which was almost at ground level in a large city street, behind the grillwork of an old Quaker cemetery. We wandered through the shop of Betsy Ross who embroidered the first Stars and Stripes. A national fundraising campaign had made it possible to buy this old shop to conserve it along with the spinning wheel and loom, as the national cradle of American glory. I would like to say more about everything we saw and experienced, but it is a bit beyond my subject.

With the local train we arrived at the home of our host well before the return of his wife. He lived in Tioga, a cheery new suburb, and had a comfortable two-story house, separated from the street by a veranda and a bit of lawn. Rows of houses, all the same model, went down both sides of the wide, shady streets.

Eugène Graff and I were the guests of the minister, and Pilet and Olivier would be those of Mrs. Syle, but in her absence Rev. Dantzer made arrangements for them with his charming daughter, who also knew French.

We waited in the cool night air under the electric lamps, sitting in those comfortable rocking chairs that are part of all American home furnishings. The minister's youngest son came to call with his wife. As he knew sign language, as do all the children of the deaf in America, he could easily chat with us. He spoke of his love for France, that he had not been affected by the draft, but that his older brother who was away on a trip would most likely be called up.

In the middle of this conversation Mrs. Dantzer returned and was very surprised to see us there. But in a few moments she had arranged bed and bath for us. With the torrid heat of the United States and the fatigue it causes, a bath before bed is considered a good restorative. Mrs. Dantzer was a wonderful homemaker and did everything herself. Thanks to her and her care, her cooking and baking skills, we were in a way initiated into American family life. We tasted unknown dishes, with old-fashioned ingredients that have been forgotten in France, such as molasses to sweeten tea or her pound cake. We take this opportunity to express the gratitude of travelers who have kept a sweet memory of the kind hostess of a distant country who softened their exile.

I would imagine that Pilet and Olivier were similarly well treated by Mrs. Syle. But as I said earlier, Olivier had developed a case of laryngitis in the oven-like halls of the Goodyear plant in Akron. Mrs. Syle took him to a female doctor who prescribed just the right medication and he recovered as if by magic.

Rev. Dantzer's family was of French origin, or more exactly was from Alsace-Lorraine. His father and several members of his family emigrated to America when Germany annexed their small homeland. From his family connections, he retained some knowledge of French and was able to understand us. But since he had received his elementary education in America he was much stronger in English. As his family was Catholic he began his studies with the nuns of the Le Couteulx Sainte-Marie Institution in Buffalo. Then he went on to Gallaudet College in Washington. He became one of Edward Miner Gallaudet's best students, and received his degree there. As he wished to devote his life to pastoral work among his fellow deaf, he converted to the Protestant religion and joined the Episcopalian church. He studied theology, received his degree, and was ordained.

Conversation with him revealed him to be one of the elite, well educated but modest, jolly and witty. His features were stamped with his smiling kindness.

All Soul Eve Reception

A good crowd had turned out. There was applause, clouds of waving handkerchiefs after the Rev. Dantzer had introduced us. He signed a speech full of compliments which we found extremely kind. We, in turn, one after the other, expressed our thanks, identified areas where French and American opinions converged, offered comparisons between the American and French deaf, spoke of the century-long friendship, of the Gallaudets, the Clercs. We praised the All Souls' Church, its pastor, the charitable works of the Philadelphia deaf, the home for the elderly, Mr. Lit who had insisted on coming along, something he did only rarely. M. Olivier, in turn, emphasized the bombing of Rheims and German aggression in his remarks. He made a strong impression.

Then, leaving the platform, we had to shake more than a hundred hands. People lined up to pass in front of us. I had the pleasure of again seeing deaf people whom I had met in 1893 and in particular to discover our fellow-countryman, Henri Rose, who had been in Philadelphia for almost twenty-five years and whom I had first met in 1893. He was a former pupil of the school in Ronchin-lez-Lille and was from the French-speaking part of Flanders. He was a shoemaker and earned a good living. He liked his life well enough but expressed annoyance at losing his proficiency in French for lack of reading material. We signed him up as a new subscriber to the *Gazette*.

We were offered ice cream and other refreshments. We chatted with one group of people and then another. Young women asked us anxiously if we were afraid of submarines and balked at the idea of returning home. I replied that our last hour is written in God's book and that we would have to put our trust in Him, that I could just as surely be killed in the streets by an automobile while distracted by looking at pretty young women like them. They laughed and said that I was funny and that they would pray for our safe return. I kissed the hands of several of them by way of farewell.

Home for Aged

That Sunday afternoon, Rev. Dantzer had suggested that we might go to the Philadelphia suburb of Doylestown, to visit the Home for Aged and Infirm Deaf. We were quick to accept his offer. This is a matter of great social importance for our little world. In 1893, with my companion Chazal, I had visited the home in Poughkeepsie in New York State, and on this trip time had been too short for us to stop there on our way to Albany. It was then of real interest for us to examine at first hand another instance of one of the most useful American innovations for the improvement of the lot of the deaf.

Doylestown is thirty-five miles to the north of Philadelphia. We took the local railway as far as Willow Grove and then switched to another. But on that fine summer Sunday, the crowds were enormous, all the more so as Willow Grove was a popular Sunday excursion destination and hordes of people got on and off at every stop. It was a long but rapid trip and the landscape was charming and picturesque. After the crowded and bustling city the tracks led us into the countryside with huge green fields and model farmhouses here and there. There were summer cottages in the groves of trees. Then we reached Doylestown, a prosperous little town, made up mostly of one-story houses, gathered around a monument erected in memory of the heroes of the War of Independence.

A short stroll on foot and we were in front of the Home for the Aged and Infirm Deaf, situated in the middle of grounds with lawns and flowerbeds in the English style. The building, short, rather massive, and in the English architectural style, crouched under a blue-green tapestry of ivy. A veranda, a roofed gallery open to the air, ran along the front of the building. We saw the pensioners sitting in their rocking chairs, in conversation with Pilet and Olivier who had arrived before us in the company of Mrs. Syle.

We were given a friendly reception by the hearing administrators of the home, Mr. John Vandegrift, the superintendent, and Mrs. Sarah S. Vandegrift, the matron. Their intelligent and active devotion assures that the home fully meets its objectives of care and support.

We shook hands with the retirees. There were about twenty of them and women were more numerous than men. Many had white hair. The only somewhat younger person was crippled. Their questions, their observations about France, about the German aggression gave proof that their intelligence was still sound. They all seemed spry and in good health. They said that they were happy in the home, at rest from the burden of years, well treated and well cared for. In short, we had no reason to be concerned for their situation. But we were struck by the melancholy thought that humanity of which we are a part, after having enjoyed young and strong bodies, is condemned in old age to a resigned inactivity that makes the day too long and the night too short, until implacable Death comes to draw you down to the depth of nonexistence. What consoled all those people in that antechamber to death was their religious faith, their certitude of a future life with Jesus in the heavenly city. Their piety, although Protestant, could not have been more exemplary. I cannot see why God, worshipped in so many diverse religions, would not be compassionate toward us poor humans, cradled in the hope that we place in Him from all the points of the earth. Nonetheless, I envy the elderly who have had the chance, in part thanks to their own self-knowledge, to keep themselves in fit and robust good health and who work, keep themselves occupied, continue to learn, seeking the best possible future until the last minute and the final great sleep.

But our hearts were to be gripped by a spectacle that was, however, not entirely new to us. It was impossible for a sensitive heart to remain unmoved by it. As we entered the common room we met eight blind and deaf women. They were seated in armchairs, sitting straight and proper, well enough dressed in white blouses and dark skirts, with Braille books on their knees. Their hair was white, their cheeks full and pink, suggesting good health, but their eyes were closed, half-closed, or veiled. Living tombs, I thought to myself, more than walled up. I went up to one of them and I put my right hand under her nimble fingers, soft and well cared for, and I fingerspelled "I am French" and then I pressed her two hands in a rush of fraternal feeling. Her face, that had seemed so dead, brightened in surprise and a smile came to her lips. She signed, "You are French. Hello." Then she nodded her head as if in amazement, not able to say anything more, her pupils fixing me telepathically from behind the permanent closure of her lids. I withdrew, taken aback. This woman had once been beautiful and then an illness that accompanied old age had closed her eyes to the light of admiring looks. Three sisters were pointed out to me, all deaf, who had gone blind one after another, at almost the same advanced age. There is a terrible fatality, but there is also extraordinary resignation. Perhaps one can find a natural rationale, as did the sublime Helen Keller, for having lost one's hearing, sight, and speech at a young age. But to be afflicted with blindness after having lived a deaf life with courage was truly proof of fate's cruelty.

This, as much as anything we saw, made evident the great usefulness of such a humane and charitable institution as the home.

The Home for Aged and Infirm Deaf was founded on November 24, 1902, by the Pennsylvania Association for the Advancement of the Deaf. This realized a motion passed as early as 1891.

And it was the association that supported the home. It had never received any assistance from the state. Voluntary contributions, gifts, legacies, holiday events, charity sales, all contribute to its upkeep. Its capital fund, as of May 31, 1913, amounted to about $7,000. Its goal was to build up a capital of $50,000. The land was valued at $22,000. The operating fund amounted to between $1,000 and $1,200.

The financial report for 1913 showed revenues of $5,325.45, of which almost $1,000 were paid by the pensioners, and expenses of $3,679.22. One can see that this was not a capital-intensive operation and this should encourage those in France who dream of establishing a similarly much needed home for our aged deaf.

It is remarkable that the superintendent and his wife are satisfied with a combined salary of $765. This is a level of denial that was unknown to me, given the high salaries that are general in the United States.

To these revenues are to be added gifts in kind that are made by charitable people of the neighborhood: baskets of strawberries, cherries, rhubarb, pears, apples, tomatoes, corn, oats, potatoes, jam, towels, linen, and so on. The Lord's tithe: He who gives to the poor, loans to God.

In addition, the establishment was furnished with goods from legacies or with items that the pensioners had brought with them and that would be left to the home on their death.

Admission to the home was regulated by certain rules and precautions. In principle, it was left to the board of trustees, whose chairman was Mr. Crouter, the principal of the institution at Mount Airy. The Pennsylvania deaf who are able to pay make a contribution of about $160, while those from other states pay $200. The blind deaf pay an additional $50. Those without financial resources may be exempted from all payment.

But a physician examines all candidates for admission. He will not accept the incurably ill, nor those with infectious or contagious diseases, nor the insane, senile, or feebleminded, nor those with behavorial problems. A six-month trial period is obligatory. If the results are not satisfactory, the applicant is returned to his or her family or, in the case of mental deficiency, to a special hospital designed for hearing patients. And that's that.

These are very sound principles. And the good mental and physical health of the present pensioners is the proof of it.

A visit to the rooms offered none of the sights that might be expected in a hospice. These were quite simply family rooms. But the arrangement of the furniture betrayed its very diverse origins, from so many people with different tastes. Some of the rooms, with their neat beds, perhaps a little too close together, did, however, give an impression of order. The rooms bore the names of those who had contributed to outfitting them or supporting them. Thus we could read inscribed on a banner the names of Mr. and Mrs. Hayman, two wealthy deaf persons from New York, who were recently deceased but had honored our bicentenary congress for the Abbé de l'Épée in Paris in 1912.

The Lit Brothers Department Store

Almost all of Monday was spent looking at the sights of the city.

But I did have one wish: to pay a visit to a young oral deaf man, Mr. Lit, whom I had known in Paris, which he visited on two occasions. I knew that his uncle and father had a department store.

And indeed we had passed in front of it and remarked that it was almost as long and fine as the Samaritaine stores in Paris.

Mrs. Syle said that Mr. Lit was perhaps in his office. She went up to ask while we made a few small purchases in one of the departments. When she came back it was to tell us to get back in the elevator with her. We went up to the top floor, close to the air and light, and we were shown into a large modern office. Soon Mr. Lit came up with his hands outstretched, affable and welcoming. He was acquainted only with me and just barely remembered Olivier from a banquet in Rheims. The people he generally sought out in Paris were the Spanish painters from Zubiaurre, the sculptors of statues, Ebstein and Mauduit. He was charmed and surprised by the visit of the French deaf and made us stay for lunch.

We ate in the store's large restaurant, which took up most
of the upper floor. There were countless round tables, with white
tablecloths, fine china, an extremely varied menu with different
price combinations, tasty and abundant dishes, and cold and hot
drinks. Our department stores have still not hit on this idea, and
yet it is so convenient. And they did things even better than our
fashionable eating spots. For here there was not only a luxury
restaurant, there was also a buffet for quicker, simpler meals, and
a place to serve yourself coffee and tea. They had everything. It
was as comfortable as you could hope for, and I'm sure it was
quite profitable. Mr. Lit would offer proof of this when he took
us behind the scenes of the department store.

The store's business is based above all on providing credit,
a bit like Dufayel in France. This entails a fairly complex bookkeeping operation, given the number of parties, departments,
sections, subsections, typists, stockers, receivers, accountants,
etc. who are involved. Yet Mr. Lit, calm and cool but
good-humored toward us, passed through this beehive, greeted
cordially or respectfully depending on how close the employees
were to him. He explained to us in very clear signs, showed us
the books, had the accounting work performed under our eyes,
showed us the installment payments, the revenues, the outstanding accounts, all grouped according to the product range.
"These are the assets," he said, "and these are the debits, an
area I don't want to get into, don't want to think about, something I just hate." Thus this enormous apparatus of files and
accounts was simplified for us. On the assets side were the services for receiving goods, stocking, invoices from suppliers, bills
to be paid, everything that came from the factories to be sold
here in turn. Visiting each of these functions took us more than
an hour.

We thought it was useless to walk through the departments.
They were all organized in the same way. The elevator took us
down to the basement. This was a continuation of the animated
master plan we had seen upstairs. Shipping and delivery offices,
goods leaving the store, here too things were mechanized. Parcels

and packages slid past on conveyor belts, going up or down, crossing one another. This was the invention of the deaf Mr. Lit. Then the parcels passed in front of a group of employees who picked them up, checked to see whether they were addressed to customers in good standing, and then put them aside or sent them on their way. Then at the end of the belt were the deliverymen who took the packages and classified them according to which truck was to take them. Thus, a purchase made at two o'clock in the afternoon would be delivered to your home by five or six. However, checking the labels is a very demanding business, since there are thousands of people just with the name Schmidt.

Here was simplicity in the midst of complexity. And this young deaf man who went about, undisturbed but at home, surrounded by a multitude of employees, in this labyrinth of services, astonished us. He is up to date on everything because he also works in the administration. His uncle heads the enterprise, assisted by his father. Lit and his cousins complete the team. Thus everything works well because the family gets along and takes into account the talents of each of its members. In addition, they are Jewish and thus both practical and hard-working. But Jewish Americans, as I have already said, have fewer prejudices about the deaf than French Jews. I know a deaf Jew in Paris whose family also has a store selling goods on credit, but it is much smaller than the Lits' operation. Well, this young deaf man, who worked for the company, had none of the unfettered, enterprising spirit or aptitude and initiative that we so admired in Mr. Lit, who possessed all the characteristics of the American businessman, one well able to run his own affairs.

Mr. Lit was a former pupil of the Mount Airy Institution. He speaks and reads lips with ease. When he was in Paris, the granddaughter of Pereire, Mme Halphen, whose salon he frequented, was astonished and captivated by him.

The example of Mr. Lit should inspire the teachers of deaf children who come from wealthy families of industrialists. There is no need to whine over the fact that the child can neither speak nor hear. Give him rational and lively instruction, develop his will, stimulate his ambition, encourage him to disregard prejudice, build up his courage, and you will create a man who does honor to his family instead of being a good-for-nothing parasite, living more or less wisely off his inheritance.

Mt. Airy School

On the morning of Tuesday, July 24, we were at the school for the deaf at the agreed hour. Mr. A. L. E. Crouter was there waiting for us and gave us the same cordial welcome as the day previous. He offered us refreshments, some delicious iced ginger ale and excellent cigars, and we chatted. Although he was one of the foremost oralists in North America, Mr. Crouter was a master signer. He signed clearly and fingerspelled distinctly. In fact, at heart he was a combined method man, but was attracted to getting as much from the oral method as possible. At Mount Airy, speech and lipreading are given particular attention, especially in the primary and intermediate departments. These sections have been put in the charge of women teachers, eighteen in each department, with Mrs. Suzanne E. Bliss and Mrs. Louise Upham as their respective head teachers. In the advanced department, where Mr. Manning is the head teacher, there are five male teachers and twelve female.

Mr. Crouter gave us a copy of the institutional report for 1917, an interesting brochure of 120 pages, with very well executed photographs. He said that the institution, founded in 1820, would naturally be celebrating its centenary in two years time and he hoped, particularly if the war were over, to invite teachers and deaf people from Europe who would receive a worthy reception in Philadelphia, the city of brotherly love.

I had already met Mr. Crouter several times, in Chicago, Edinburgh, and Paris. I always found him the same: active and youthful despite his white hair. Looking at him, I comforted myself with the hope that he would be able to achieve what he

had conceived. Yet, shortly after our departure, he fell rather seri-
ously ill. Devoted care and his robust constitution put him back
on his feet after a short time. May he find in his recovered health
fresh vigor to pursue his work for the advancement of the deaf
and to be present at the ultimate triumph of his school.

As it happens, the Philadelphia Institution is one of the most
important sites of deaf education in the world. It scarcely had
any pupils in 1820 and in 1831, when it was located in the center of the city, at the corner of Broad and Pine Streets. Now it
normally has about 540 pupils, of which 293 boys and 247 girls.
There are seventy-four teachers, thirty-one administrators, and
a staff of eighty-eight, that is a total family of no fewer than 733
persons.

The bursaries are paid by the state of Pennsylvania and have
been awarded to 210 regular pupils and two special cases. The
state of Delaware supports six pupils and the institution itself
another six through grants from its foundation. Only sixteen
pupils are paying full cost of their room and board.

The financial report shows revenues of $184,784.30 and
normal expenses of $181,862.09. This too gives an indication
of the scale of operations.

The oral method is employed in all classes. Signing is permitted only during recess.

There are two deaf and blind girls who receive instruction
via the manual alphabet and writing in Braille. The girls have
made almost phenomenal progress since entering the school.

Three pupils who received graduation diplomas from the
advanced section have been admitted to Gallaudet College in
Washington. Two others went to post-secondary institutions in
their home towns where they take courses with hearing students. Yet another, Mr. Warren M. Smaltz, obtained his bachelor of arts degree after graduating from the Central High School
in Philadelphia, placing third among 139 graduating college students. As this young man, who is such a striking example of what
a deaf person can achieve when he can speak and read lips, is
also quite poor, he has been made a monitor for the pupils in

the advanced section, which then permits him to take correspondence courses from the University of Chicago. Perhaps he will eventually devote his career to teaching his fellow-deaf, for in the United States, despite the dominance of the oral method, the assistance of deaf instructors is not scorned. There have always been some on the teaching staff at Mount Airy. We had the pleasure, at the home of Mr. Sanders, of dining with a speaking deaf elementary teacher who was as cultivated as she was charming.

To return to Mr. Schmaltz, I should point out that in an open competition sponsored by the League of the American School for Peace on the subject of "The Influence of the United States in Advancing the Cause of World Peace" he carried off third prize.

In addition to the classics, the pupils read a large number of magazines, scientific or literary journals, even daily newspapers. It is reading, and this can not be stressed too much, that enhances the knowledge of the deaf. And by permitting its pupils to read general publications, Mount Airy, like other American institutions, advances their knowledge of life and its problems. The institution's own annual report makes this very point.

Classes are held in the advanced section in the mornings and the afternoons are devoted to industrial training.

The industrial section is under the supervision of Mr. Joseph J. Baily. It has fourteen sections: baking (nine pupils), masonry (ten), cabinet-making (thirty-six), furniture repair (eight), gardening and greenhouses (five), laundry (sixteen), home economics (forty), dressmaking (144), painting and varnishing (?), glazing (eight), typography and printing (thirty-two), shoe-making (twenty-eight), tailoring (thirty-five), dress-making (twenty-four) and general seamstress work (twenty-three).

The printing shop is under the supervision of Mr. Arthur J. Godwin. It is very well equipped, and has a linotype machine and a large cylindrical press. The young pupils who work with these machines become very skillful operators, as they are called there. A sixteen-page newspaper, artistically laid out and illustrated with good photographs, is published twice a month. This is the *Mount Airy World*, whose editor is Mr. J. A. Weaver. Its objective is naturally to teach all aspects of the art of publishing to the apprentice typographers. It is also a means of communication between pupils and their parents, a way as well to maintain contact between former pupils and the school, and a way to furnish pupils with articles of interest, from the most simple to the most advanced. Thus, in an issue taken at random, I found this memory poem.

> Snow in January
> Ice in February
> Wind in March
> Rain in April
> Buds in May
> Roses in June
> Play in July
> Warm days in August
> School in September
> Apples in October
> Cold days in November
> Christmas in December.

There were also notes about pupils and their doings, and articles in defense of the deaf. "The deaf are not defectives." There were reports on sporting events, bits of news about former pupils and how they were making out in life, reports on American soldiers of fortune engaged in earlier conflicts.

The three instructional sections are separate, each in its fine set of buildings in the midst of fine lawns. The infirmary is also at some distance from the other buildings. I had already seen all this in 1893 when it was all quite new. Now the buildings have lost their new look and have some of the authority that comes with age. The interiors do not seem to have changed all that much. But we did not have a great deal of time. We had to content ourselves with a quick visit to the main hall. As well, the pupils had left for the summer holidays.

We thanked and warmly congratulated Mr. Crouter, and those teachers who were present. Rev. Dantzer, who had accompanied us, took us to a restaurant in Germantown and invited us to a farewell lunch, then went with us to the station where we were to board the train for Washington. With a great deal of emotion and regret we said goodbye to this exceptional clergyman, this oral deaf gentleman, generous, learned, who is an honor to his ministry and well as to the whole deaf community.

WASHINGTON, D.C.
What the Deaf Are Capable Of

The Reception

When the train brought the French delegation to the capital of the United States on the evening of Monday, July 23, a group of deaf gentlemen were waiting at the station. Among them were Messrs. Hannan, Pfunder, Rev. Merril, Stewart, and others. Our reception was all the more enthusiastic since Mr. Hannan had lived for some time in Paris, while completing his training as a sculptor and he had conveyed to his companions his eagerness to welcome representatives from France.

But first we hurried to a small restaurant where we were able to get some refreshments.

As night fell, along wide streets lined with new one-story homes we made our way to the celebrated spot where every deaf person must go on his arrival in Washington, to Gallaudet College, the national college for the deaf, of which we shall have a great deal more to say in the following.

It has the appearance of a large park. On our arrival, a private detective came up out of the dark and, recognizing us as deaf, then disappeared among the trees. Public places everywhere are now being so guarded, we were told, because of the war.

With their elegant and unencumbered architecture, the college buildings had retained the appearance that I had known twenty-five years earlier. Some were however surrounded by scaffolding.

But the statue of Gallaudet seemed to me to have been moved. Instead of facing away from the front of the main building, it is now opposite on a small plot of dry grass that burned with thousands of unexpected, motionless spots of fire. Our hosts explained to us that these were fireflies. This was quite a new spectacle for us. Set off against the dull light from the glowering sky this illumination at ground level had a very charming effect. We thought of the pleasant hours that the students of the college must spend in this captivating setting, provided they had some feeling for the beauties of nature.

Two deaf professors were there to greet us, Messrs. Hotchkiss and Drake, and they informed us that the principal of the college, Mr. Percival Hall, would receive us the next evening when we would be his guests. We drew up our schedule for the following day, and then were accompanied to the streetcar.

Vaudeville and President Wilson

But we scarcely had the means to remain longer with our Washington friends, among whom I must mention the charming ladies whose smiles and wit were reason enough to wish to stay. But President Hall urged us on. Out in the night an impressive automobile was waiting for us and we got in without having much of an idea of just where he was taking us. But Graff made a guess and was soon proven right. The car stopped in front of a building festooned with lights. It was a vaudeville theater. President Hall ushered us to seats in the first row of the balcony. On the stage was a chorus line of slim and pretty young women. Their dancing was varied and captivating, with high kicks and bold turns. But President Hall pointed out someone sitting in the same row as we were, four or five persons to our right.

It was President Wilson!

We were immensely grateful to President Hall for having arranged this wonderful surprise.

It was the chance of a lifetime and a source of joy to a Frenchman interested in philosophical reflection to have the opportunity to study one of the great figures of our times, the master of the future that would see the triumph of human liberty and justice, and the elimination of the wars to which a contagious madness had inspired humankind.

There he was, simple and modest, along with Mrs. Wilson, a charming and cultivated woman. He was in the company of a friend, and naturally had other people both behind and below him. Thus he seemed the true representative of the people, disdaining the costly and burlesque grandeur of the rulers and heads of state of Europe and Asia. He looked on, amused by the graceful antics of the dancing girls. Thus had President Wilson shed his weighty preoccupations and showed himself to be very human, dispelling the impression of narrow Puritanism that we had of him in France.

He is a man, neither more nor less. He is of so much greater worth than a laughable superman who is indifferent to the real fate of the world. President Wilson stayed out of the conflict for a long time because, from his superior vantage point, he wished to understand the causes, reasons, and objectives. When his reason was enlightened, he did not hesitate to take sides. And his people with him. And now the formidable force of the United States is readying itself to come to the rescue of France, which for three years has held off the renewed rush of the Huns with its valor.

Looking at President Wilson, we French deaf felt reassured of the future of our beloved country, of civilization, and of the world. Were it not for our concern for protocol, which has its value, we would have gone over and written on our notepads, just as our compatriot Laurent Clerc used to do to converse in writing with President Monroe.

When the show was over, President Wilson calmly left the theater. Everyone followed his departure with their eyes. It was simple and it was sufficient.

President Hall took us to his club where in a quiet room he offered us an excellent French wine chilled with ice and a light supper. Then his car took us back to Kendall Green where two student rooms had been made up for us. We slept so well there that we imagined that we too had become students at Gallaudet College.

Gallaudet College

Waking the next morning, Wednesday, July 25, around six o'clock, we quickly grasped what the life of a student at the college was like.

Our room was bright and roomy. It held two beds, two small dressers with drawers and shelves for each student to set out his books, and a large desk where a student could read or write. Thus, students are housed by twos, the boys in one building, and the girls in another some distance away. But they take their classes together, in the same room and with the same professor. This is American coeducation, which produces results of a high moral order that is unknown in Europe.

Each bathroom is designed for four students. There are sinks with hot and cold water and cold showers. The young men can then shave and comb their hair at their leisure. And, in fact, we ran into one of them whose parents lived in the far West and who continued his studies through the summer. He gave us all kinds of interesting detailed information about Gallaudet.

At seven o'clock we went to have breakfast with President Hall. The meal was abundant, freshly prepared, and delicious.

Then our visit to the institution began. In his huge, well lit office, Mr. Hall showed us the registrar's files, both old and new, where we could examine the grades and degrees awarded to students, and even look over their curricula vitae, what they did with their lives after graduating from college. There was information on the causes of their deafness, and on their parents. We noted that the new tables were much more scientifically conceived than the old ones.

The president was also kind enough to give us numerous photographs and documents relating to the college, which were extremely interesting.

To really understand the college, sense its true life, and appreciate the high quality of its teaching, it must be visited during the academic year, ideally several times. One would also have to attend the classes given by the professors. Even more would be necessary, for example, to gain access to the secret societies the students have formed, the Kappa Gamma Fraternity for young men, the Owls for young women. One would have to saturate oneself with the whole college atmosphere.

At the cinema showing in Hartford we had seen scenes from college life, in particular the events of Presentation Day when students who were graduating walked past in single file in the caps and gowns. This vision haunted us, and we wanted to witness it for ourselves. But now it was empty everywhere. Buildings were being renovated under the direction of an architect and an engineer, for in the United States not even the smallest construction project is undertaken without both being present.

With President Hall we climbed over the broken plaster and under the beams, slipping and bending, and we could see that the young ladies and lady teachers would have fashionable little rooms waiting for them, quite up to date as they say. On our way we met the college carpenter working at his bench on the landing of some stairs. He was deaf. He said that he had sent one of his sons off to the war. For France, he signed.

Some of the classrooms held only chairs in front of a blackboard. These were lecture rooms and to do their work the students have desks in their rooms.

In the chapel, which also serves as a conference hall, the floor was empty—no benches, no chairs. The busts along the walls were draped in cloth. There were likenesses of the Abbé de l'Épée, Abbé Sicard, President Garfield, assassinated by a madman and before that a great friend of the deaf. There we also saw a replica of the medallion of Pastor Thomas Gallaudet, the son, which had been executed by our friend the sculptor Hannan. And outside, at the entrance, an immense bust of the Abbé de l'Épée, a gift of the deaf French sculptor Felix Plessis, who was one of the six members of the first delegation in 1893.

In the building for industrial apprenticeship, the chemistry classroom and the laboratories caught our attention. Gallaudet College has well understood that chemistry is a science eminently accessible to the intelligent deaf. In the silence in which they concentrate, they can carry out the most detailed analyses, and discover the most useful combinations of elements. Thus quite a number of expert chemists have graduated from Gallaudet. One of them, President Hall assured us, was reported to earn $10,000 a year or about 50,000 francs. Poor us!

The patron of Gallaudet College is the president of the United States, Mr. Woodrow Wilson, assisted by a corporation consisting of a senator and two members of Congress.

There is a faculty of seventeen persons, with Edward Miner Gallaudet as president emeritus and Percival Hall as the serving president. Mr. Hall is also a professor of pedagogy and applied mathematics. The vice president is Mr. Edward A. Fay, a professor of languages. Then come J. Burton Hotchkiss, professor of English and philosophy; Amos G. Draper, professor of mathematics and Latin; Ch. R. Ely, professor of natural sciences; H. E. Day, professor of English and history; Isaac Allison, professor of mathematics and mechanics; Elizabeth Peet, associate professor of Latin and head of the college for girls; Helen Northrop, instructor in mathematics and English; V. O. Skyberg, lecturer in Latin and natural science; F. H. Hughes, instructor in mathematics and physics; H. D. Drake, instructor in agriculture; I. S. Fussfeld, instructor in English and history; A. D. Bryant, instructor in drawing; Agnes Suman, instructor in home economics; and Helen Devreaux, gymnastics instructor.

In addition, there is a section for speech and for the training of hearing students who plan to become teachers of the deaf. Percival Hall is in charge of these sections, assisted by Annie E. Jameson and Sarah H. Porter.

There are five classes of students.

During the 1916–1917 school year there were 107 students, of which sixty-five are young men and forty-two young women. Of these, ten are seniors, eighteen juniors, thirteen sophomores, fifteen freshmen, six special students, and forty-five preparatory students.

They come from the principal American institutions for the deaf and are admitted only after an examination. Students may be dropped from the preparatory year. The full curriculum comprises five years of study, and each academic year is divided into three terms.

The system of instruction that is employed consists of reports on assigned subjects, discussions, and open lectures; work in laboratories with instruments; reading assignments; and English composition.

Instruction in spoken English and via lipreading is available to students on all levels. Special measures are taken to preserve and enhance, through recurrent useful exercises, any degree of competence in speech and lipreading that a student may have when admitted to the college. Naturally, the use of sign language and fingerspelling can in no way negatively affect this instruction.

By visits to the Library of Congress, to the collections of the Smithsonian Institution, the National Museum, the Corcoran Gallery, and other such public institutions, the students have priceless means to increase their knowledge.

The curriculum includes among other subjects plane geometry; algebra; Latin; history (antiquity, Middle Ages, modern period, American); English composition; commerce and finance; physics, chemistry and chemical analysis; English literature; agriculture or home economics; French and German philology; physiology, zoology; electricity, mechanics; ethics and political science; astronomy, mineralogy and geology; the basics of law, government, international law; logic and psychology. All of these advance in degree of complexity as students move to higher classes. Thus Latin is taught during the preparatory year but French is offered only to fourth year students, German to fifth year students, etc. Since we have met a fair number of former students who write French more or less competently, we are led to believe that the teaching of our language is carried out in serious fashion. Yet I would have to say that it was among the generation around 1878–1886, the "'78–'86ers" as they say at the college, that I met students with the best knowledge of French, such as Draper, Gray, George, and Hodgson.

In addition to these subjects, which are more or less compulsory, there are optional subjects, the most important of which relate to chemistry and mathematics, applied electricity (generators, motors), dairy and poultry farming, and home economics.

Hearing students in the teacher training program are enrolled for three terms during the year. They are brought up to date both theoretically and practically in all the methods of teaching the deaf: sign language, fingerspelling, speech, writing. They live in residence with the college students and assist the teachers at the Kendall School, of which I will have more to say below, in the supervision of the younger pupils. Thus, they have insight into the mentality of the deaf, both young and somewhat older.

Finding them jobs is an easy matter, since schools in need of teachers have only to get in touch with the college.

The timetable for classes and study periods is 8 to 9 a.m., 9:15 a.m. to 12:15 p.m., 1:30 to 3:30 p.m., and 7:30 to 10 p.m. (except Friday evening), and Saturday morning from 9 to 11:30 a.m. Each morning, except Saturday, there is a service at the chapel at 9 a.m., and a supplementary service at 5 p.m. in the afternoons on Sundays. These religious services are of a nondenominational character, that is, they scrupulously respect the religion of each student, leaving them free to seek out the clergy of their choice outside the college.

The students are all members of the YMCA, which is currently doing so much good, both moral and material, for war victims.

There are no college uniforms. Students develop the habit of dressing suitably, as one would for regular work. The college provides a laundry service, as well as bedclothes and towels.

As is proper in America, physical education is systematically organized in a gymnasium equipped with everything that might be needed. In addition the following sports are practiced: football, in particular, and track and field, baseball, basketball, even wrestling and boxing. For the young women, there is tennis and open-air exercises.

The students have created societies, some of them secret, although there is faculty insight into activities, the others public. There is a literary society and two drama societies, one for men and the other for women. Private performances are given on Saturday evenings and there are one or two public performances in the course of the year.

The students have a magazine, the *Buff and Blue*, named after the school colors. It appears monthly and its thirty-two pages are edited by students under the guidance of their professors. A portion of the magazine is reserved for the alumni. The best and most novel of their contributions, including poetry by those who have the gift, are published here.

Need I add that the editor-in-chief of the *American Annals of the Deaf*, the best journal in the world devoted to our special pedagogical mission, Mr. E. A. Fay, is one of the most distinguished professors at the college and also one of the best friends of the deaf?

Each student, when admitted to the college, is put under the supervision of a professor, his advisor, who is a kind of intellectual godfather and whom he can consult as he would a parent or older brother.

The college corporation has been authorized by an act of Congress to confer degrees in the arts and sciences just as they are awarded at other colleges. The degree of bachelor of arts is conferred on students who have successfully concluded a complete four-year academic course. The degree of bachelor of science is conferred on those who have successfully completed two years of general studies and two years of science studies at the advanced level, four years in all. Students are allowed to take special courses that lead to the degrees of bachelor of philosophy or of letters. A master's degree is available to graduates who during a minimum three-year program have given proof of their substantive progress in science, philosophy, literature, or liberal arts since their graduation. The degree of bachelor of education is awarded to graduates of the teaching training program, who must have previously obtained a bachelor's degree in another subject.

The college was founded in 1864. In 1914, from June 22 to 25, it celebrated its fiftieth anniversary. On this occasion, Dr. Hotchkiss observed in his address that during its fifty years of existence 1,232 young men and women had matriculated at the college, of which 478 or 39 percent had received degrees. Of the total number, 1,216 had come from the forty-seven United States and territories, eleven from Canada, and five from Great Britain. The first deaf person to be awarded a bachelor's degree was the painter John Carlin, who then proved to be a great supporter of the college. Since then, 536 degrees have been awarded to 505 persons, 367 receiving these degrees on completion of their undergraduate studies, while forty-seven received master's degrees by pursuing advanced studies. Teacher trainees were awarded eighty-one bachelor of education degrees. In addition to all this, the college conferred sixty-one honorary degrees, exclusively to persons who had distinguished themselves by their efforts to advance the cause of the deaf.

As you can see, Gallaudet College has made an enormous contribution to progress in deaf education and has restored self-respect to many in the deaf community. It has also shown the hearing world what the deaf are capable of when they set themselves to study, work, and confront obstacles.

One of the alumnae of the college, Mrs. Sylvia Chaplin Balis, said in her speech at the fiftieth anniversary celebrations:

The half educated look up to their better educated fellows and follow willingly in their wake. They rely upon them for guidance, advice, and leadership. In many cases their confidence is not misplaced.

A college graduate, if so disposed, can organize his fellows and hold them in united fellowship, and with their assistance maintain and carry to a consummation almost any scheme that aims to the betterment of the deaf as a class.

Their minds are well trained, their reasoning powers developed and they usually have more self-control as well as a clearer insight and broader understanding of many topics and affairs that affect the individual or national interests. The college graduate has proven to the world the abilities of the deaf, the possibilities that lie within their grasp, the power of will and intellect over physical defect.

They have put heart into their less courageous comrades and have led them onward and upward out of the dimness and gloom of a gray existence into the light and happiness of higher aims. They have led them along paths of knowledge and placed within their groping hands the key that opens the door of opportunity. Some of them devote all their leisure to the betterment of their less fortunate comrades.

It would take too long to detail the impressive employment opportunities that former students of the college have attained. I would recall the speech read by Mr. Hodgson at the Hartford Convention (see above), which provides an edifying list of such successful graduates.

Yet in some deaf circles, I have seen criticism. They claim that the college produces sterile fruit, persons incapable of earning a living as successfully as a tradesman or artisan might. But the colleges for hearing also produce misfits. All of this proves nothing except that one ought perhaps to revise somewhat the curriculum at Gallaudet College. It would seem that this is also the view of the alumni association since in the same speech noted above Mrs. Balis expressed herself as follows:

The educational trend of the times is to shorten, not to lengthen, the period of education, to eliminate the superfluous, and reduce waste, and increase efficiency. It is becoming a question of educating to the greatest profit and in the least time those who must enter into the economic struggle. Many of them are poor and cannot spend years upon the nonessentials . . .

The youths of strongest will and most independence are the ones to see the need of a higher education.

The greatest mistake of the colleges, I think, has been their failure to educate for the practical, in money-making to educate for a living; they have leaned too far toward the idealistic in education. It is a poor education that teaches the comprehension of living but fails to show how to earn the daily bread. It is like a course in domestic science which gives all the components of the egg, but fails to show how to procure the egg, and then how to cook it.

It would now seem that the college's first priority is to increase practical training since, in addition to the chemistry and physics laboratories, there is an agriculture laboratory, dairy, stables, a farm, huge kitchen gardens. And there are deaf people who are themselves running large agrarian enterprises, beekeepers, farmers, stock-raisers—all these have graduated from the college and returned to family properties that they are now running successfully.

As well as hearing teachers, the college trains deaf people for teaching. But sad to say fewer and fewer deaf young people have this prospect in sight. The fact is that they find the salaries inadequate. This is true even though they are still above what a teacher in the advanced class at the national institution in Paris receives for his efforts. Many graduates prefer to take jobs in industry where they make from five to seven dollars a day. Thus we had seen in Akron former teachers from small schools in the south or west who found greater advantage in the manufacture of tires.

The driven industrialization of America has absorbed an entire world, those who work with their hands and those who work with their heads. The college should consider establishing a form of advanced industrial training, of developing its courses in electrical and mechanical engineering, both theoretical and practical. Deaf people can become engineers as well as architects. And in France we can take pride in the deaf (but speaking) engineer Maurice Koechlin, a product of the Hugentobler school in Lyon.

But toward the conclusion of this report I will return at greater length to the question of higher education for the deaf.

To conclude our glimpse of Gallaudet College, it should be noted that former students have created an Alumni Association of Gallaudet College. Its objectives are to preserve and enhance the influence of the college; to counter influences that aim to diminish the benefits of the college; to perpetuate friendships formed during college life; and to bond together in a harmonious whole the different generations of students. The association was founded in 1889. It is administered by a president, vice president, secretary, and treasurer. It takes advantage of the triennial conventions of the NAD to hold special meetings. The last financial report to come to my attention, for the year 1914, reveals that the association took in $1,038.25 and spent $243.58, leaving a disposable fund of about $800. The association has 172 members.

The association also has a special fund named after Edward Miner Gallaudet, which amounted to $1,900 in 1914. Its purpose is to furnish loans to needy students, to promote the admission to the college of deaf students capable of drawing profit from such an education, to contribute to improvements at the college, and to award annual prizes.

The Columbia Institution

Next to the college buildings are those of the Kendall School or the Columbia Institution for the Deaf.

This is the school for the deaf that serves Washington (the District of Columbia) and the surrounding area. Although affiliated with the college, it is autonomous and is in its own right the object of public interest, since it takes in all the deaf youngsters of school age who are seeking an elementary education.

The principal, under the general supervision of President Hall, is Mr. Lyman Steed. He is assisted by a staff of teachers, the majority of whom are female, with the additional help of students from the teacher training program.

From an administrative point of view the name "Columbia Institution" applies equally well to the college with its 163 students. It is on occasion called the "Collegiate Department," while the Kendall School is the "Primary Department." The latter had forty-eight pupils in 1916. The curriculum is spread over twelve years, two of which are advanced terminal programs.

The pure oral method (speech and lipreading) dominates teaching. Sign language occurs in only an ancillary status. It is taught and learned all on its own among the pupils, without the intervention of teachers. But a teacher or teacher trainee engaged in tutoring who learned sign language and fingerspelling in the course of the teacher training program is authorized to employ sign language in special cases as well as teaching speech and lipreading.

The subjects taught are language, history, geography, arithmetic, health, physics and chemistry, general science, and civics.

Pupils in the upper grades may elect to prepare for entrance to college studies.

We visited the Kendall School building. The classrooms were bright, clean, with comfortable school furnishings. There was a drawing studio with a number of plaster molds for sculpture in the round and even a loom. Another room, long and wide, with a stage, served as chapel, lecture hall, and theater for dramatic productions.

The budget of Gallaudet College and the Kendall School on June 30, 1916, showed $100,037.10 in revenues, and $100,365.63 in expenses. This is a substantial budget as you can see. College salaries account for $21,207.13 annually. Teachers are then well paid. The United States government supports the college with an annual appropriation of $88,921.53.

The residences at Gallaudet College bring in only about $3,000. It is clear enough that the gifted deaf often come from poor families and receive bursaries. For those who pay, residence costs for room and board amount to $350 per year.

The United States Congress voted to allocate the sum of $143,000 to refurbish the girls' dormitory at the college and to support the construction of a new one. As we had seen in the course of our brief visit, new residence rooms were already being created. But building on credit is a sensitive matter and the Capitol architect was responsible for supervising the undertaking.

New York,
The Second Visit
His Magical Sleight of Hand

With the Knights of de l'Épée

On our return to the Hotel Theresa I had found among a number of letters one from the hand of Mr. Eugene Lynch, the secretary of the New York board for the society called the Knights of de l'Épée. This Roman Catholic group of the deaf had invited us to participate in their annual picnic at Ulmer Park on July 28. Since we were all Catholics as well as fellow countrymen of the glorious patron of this association, the Abbé de l'Épée, we would certainly have been delinquent if we had not accepted. But this was the day when we were scheduled to return to France. However, a telegram from the transatlantic steamship company informed us that the departure had been postponed until Monday. We then decided to spend that Saturday with our Catholic brothers.

We then set out on our way to Ulmer Park, with the help of the information on the invitation, which told us which elevated railroad to take. But this didn't help. Since we had not paid attention to getting into the right car, we missed the station where we were supposed to get off. But at the next stop, a railway employee who understood the mistake we had made allowed us to take a train back to our stop without charging an additional fee. This dropped us off where we were supposed to be. After a stroll of five blocks along the road we were at the park, which we had earlier visited on the outing with the Elect Surds.

The New York deaf certainly are faithful to their excursion spots, since the associations all seem to hold their summer celebrations in the same place. In Paris, we would have tired of returning to the same environment. As those in charge of arranging our country forays know all too well, we continuously demand to be taken to some new spot.

The advantage of Ulmer Park is that it is close to Coney Island. Those who have had enough of the meeting, especially the young people, have only to express their hurried thanks and they are quickly over in the amusement park.

We were very kindly received by the society's officers, Eugene Lynch, the president, James Constantin, Messrs. McNolly, Kiefer, Reybold, and our cordial colleague James F. Donnelly, the publisher of the *Catholic Deaf-Mute*. We also had the great pleasure of meeting our fellow publisher Mr. Hodgson, who runs *The Deaf-Mutes' Journal* and as a thorough-going journalist, impartial and eclectic in his tastes, goes to all the deaf events that he can manage. This is what I am accustomed to do in France and Mr. Hodgson has the same willingness to be an umpire at games or the judge of foot races and the like. On this occasion, the baseball game was won by the Knights over the Frats.

Mr. Wilhelm Lipgens and Mrs. Eugenie Lipgens, who are Catholics, had made a point of coming for the specific pleasure of meeting their French friends. There were also some prominent non-Catholic deaf persons who had attended out of solidarity and courtesy. What a fine example for the deaf of Paris!

There were far fewer people than at the picnic of the Elect Surds. The explanation was that the Catholics were not all there because they are divided into two factions. Those who subscribe to the newspaper *Ephpheta* and belong to the Francis-Xavier Society, including Mr. John Francis O'Brien, were notable by their absence. Moreover, during our stay in New York this group showed no interest in our presence or in interesting us in their cause. If its founder, the late Father MacCarthy, were still alive, he would certainly have acted differently. This sharpened our regrets at the premature loss of such a devoted friend of the deaf who, along with a Jewish and Protestant colleague, had been the secretary for the Abbé de l'Épée fundraising campaign.

The Knights of de l'Épée, or the National Organization of the Catholic deaf, is both a denominational and a mutual aid society. It defends the interests of deaf Catholics, sees that the religious education of deaf children is not neglected in the non-denominational schools, assists in propagandizing for the establishment of essentially Catholic institutions, and provides help to its members.

The membership fee is three dollars, and the monthly dues are fifty cents. Health insurance costs seven dollars and covers ten weeks in a given year. In the event of death, one hundred dollars is paid out to the widow or designated heir.

It would seem that this society has copied the rituals and titles of something like the Freemasons. It is, in fact, administered by a Supreme Council whose members have the title of Supreme or Grand Knight. The Supreme Knight is currently Mr. Donnelly of New York, the Supreme Secretary is Mr. Toomey of Chicago, the Supreme Treasurer, Mr. Scott of Philadelphia, the Supreme Secretary for Finance, Mr. Harrington of Scranton, the Supreme Director, Mr. Fecteau of Massachussetts, the Supreme Steward, Mr. MacDonough of Baltimore, the Supreme Chaplain, the Rev. Gilmore of Buffalo.

The society has fourteen sections or councils, in such large cities as Chicago, Philadelphia, and Baltimore. Among the officers a great many French names can be noted, Goselin, Arthur Dupont, Bilodeau, Gandreau, Damon, Serruze, etc. Each of these sections has its chaplain, and most of these are Jesuits or from the Redemptorist order. The best known of these are Fathers Mahan, Waldhaus, Quirk, Higgins, Keelan, Muth, Coakley, McQueken, Purtell, and Galvin. All are past masters of sign language.

The Knights have their own publication, *The Catholic Deaf-Mute*. This is a monthly magazine in newspaper format, printed in several columns in a small typeface. It is remarkably well edited by Mr. James Donnelly, and this shows that he is not only a devout Catholic but also a persevering and intelligent apostle of the moral and social advancement of the deaf in general.

William Lipgens

Mr. William Lipgens is well known to some of the Parisian deaf. Following the Exposition of 1900 and for more than a year afterwards he worked in Paris as a goldsmith and engraver, in particular in the studio of the famous Lalique. When his talents came to the attention of the celebrated house of Tiffany, he was engaged and transferred to New York. Now he is one of their foremost artists, producing objects for the sumptuous stores that are the pride of Fifth Avenue. He excels not only in the finished quality of his work but also in his speed of execution, his magical sleight of hand. Since he sets his own prices and these are always accepted, since it is the customer who eventually pays, he can accomplish in a few hours the equivalent of several days work for others. He is the mostly highly paid of the New York deaf. He bought himself a house in East Orange, in New Jersey. He also placed his work in prominent banks. Yet, when he disembarked in New York he had nothing. His exceptional, unique talent and his tireless work have made him what he is today.

His origins are in the German Rhineland but he quickly became a naturalized American. He was in his native city, Dusseldorf, preparing to attend the Congress in Liège, when the war broke out. Since he claimed American nationality, he was imprisoned in Germany, released, then locked up again. Finally, after numerous painful interludes, he was able to leave on a run-down Dutch ship that extorted an exaggerated sum from him and then gave him a hammock in the bottom of the hold.

From his first marriage he has a son who is in the German army. And from his second marriage he has a son in the American army. What a singular destiny that these two brothers should run the risk of meeting one another in the random events of battle and even of firing on one another! A case like this one reminds us of just how fratricidal such a war is when the world and its communities have become so international.

William Lipgens showed us that he had become a model American citizen. But without doubt he could not help letting show some feelings for his native country and for his initial upbringing. Thus he protests when people talk of annihilating the Germans. He admits that the leaders and Junkers in Berlin must bear some responsibility for events, but he doesn't insist too much on it. But he makes a point of testifying to his affection for the deaf of France, treating them as if he were a brother and an American at heart if not by birth. First, he invited us to have lunch with him in a French restaurant in New York, then to join him at his home in East Orange.

The neighboring state of New Jersey is separated from New York only by a wide arm of the Hudson River and many of the people who live there actually work in the Empire City. After having come down from the elevated railroad, we went to the pier to take the ferry, a strange steam-powered vessel that for three cents takes on passengers, who may sit or stand, automobiles, and horses and carriages. The propellers spin for ten minutes, and we are ready to disembark on the opposite shore, in front of a station where trains are waiting to go in all directions.

In New Jersey, the laws, especially marriage laws, are different from those in New York. It would appear that a woman, whether she is in the right or not, can obtain a divorce much more easily in New Jersey than in New York.

East Orange was rather far away. The trains went through several towns. We had been told to get off at the station called Ampere, in homage to the great French scientist, which was closest to the home of Mr. Lipgens. But it was on another line and we missed the scheduled departure. Thus when we did get off, we were disoriented, all the more so when the local residents contradicted each other in giving us instructions for the right way. We walked this way and that, panting and perspiring in the terrible heat, for more than an hour. We learned the lesson that when you are traveling in an unknown country and don't want to waste your time, you must keep to the hours and routes that are given to you and not go wandering off on side trips of your own. And above all, don't ask passersby for help, when they often don't know any more than you! Nonetheless, I personally didn't really regret this distraught trek. It brought me to the charming intimacy of a new suburban development set among well-kept lawns, with boulevards and rows of green trees, all lined up squarely, and strung with telegraph and power lines. It was both enchanting and monotonous.

We were finally able to discover the home of Mr. Lipgens. Even though he had left New York after us, he was on the threshold, looking up the street, worried that we might have taken a wrong turn. But Frenchmen always keep their promises, except in cases of *force majeure*. In addition, Mrs. Eugenie Lipgens who was of Belgian origin, was French by virtue of her education and her mindset and we were obliged to present to her our respects. Mrs. Lipgens had prepared a magnificent reception in our honor. Very interested in fine cuisine, she had prepared a number of half American, half European dishes, with French wine and refreshing ice water that was welcome in the oppressive heat.

Their home was well laid out, tastefully furnished, with paintings and other objects from Europe, porcelain and glass, and a luxurious dinner service. And it was not enough to be a goldsmith for other people; one has to see to one's own needs. Thus, there were many objects there that were the work of the master's own hand. He also had a home studio, on the top floor, under the torrid roof. On the walls were photos, replicas, models of pieces that he had executed in Paris, Berlin, and Amsterdam. In the drawers were medals and jewelry in gold and silver, all finely worked. William Lipgens is truly a great artist. That was the one important thing for us, and he is a credit to the deaf of all countries.

Mrs. Lipgens also has a role in all this. She had refined taste, an acute sense of the beautiful, and rare literary talents. In addition to her mother tongue, French, which she handles with distinction and wit, she is fluent in English and German, and knows some Italian and Spanish. She has traveled a great deal in Europe and America and has crossed the Atlantic almost a dozen times to go and visit her parents in Belgium, or to visit Berlin and Paris. She reads a great deal, has very good judgment, and is very skilled in lip-reading speech in the three principal languages that she has mastered. M. Landrain, a teacher at the institution for the deaf in Berchem-Saint-Agathe, near Brussels, wrote some time ago in a pedagogical journal that he had never met a speaking deaf woman with such superior gifts. Thanks to her efforts, assisted by her talent for writing, her initiative and her perseverance, she had greatly furthered her husband's career, helping him to achieve the status he merited. This example of deaf Europeans succeeding in making their fortune in the United States is certainly worth analyzing in great detail.

Marcus L. Kenner

Another businessman. But you would hardly expect it. At meetings, he seems melancholy and self-effacing. Yet he is one of the few who know how to activate the New York deaf. It is he who took the initiative to create a fundraising campaign in order to offer the French delegation a souvenir of their visit to Hartford.

He is engaged in two lines of business. He is a special agent of the New England Mutual Life Insurance Company, of Boston, the oldest insurance company in the United States, and he manages the Communal Press, a printing company that employs deaf people.

Messieurs Graff, Pilet, and I went to visit him downtown, at 137 Grand Street, near Broadway. The shop was on the third floor of an old mansion. It was rather surprising for us to find a printing operation perched so high up in a building. In Paris, such machinery is allowed only on the ground floor and in the basement.

The shop was quite similar to the one I operate in rue du Croissant: rows of dusty and darkened trays, an old desk littered with stacks of paper, boxes and leaflets, but the printing presses, the stapling and folding machines were very advanced. The workshop was wide and deep. About fifteen men worked there under normal circumstances, half deaf and half hearing. The foreman is hearing in order to facilitate relations with customers.

The works that were done there were little marvels of the typographer's art. The company had specialized in luxury publications. The *Casino* was a promotional album for the Narragansett shore in Rhode Island. It was tastefully laid out, simple but original, with photographs, framings, and floral elements placed in the most unusual way.

Among other publications, Marcus Kenner prints *The Jewish Deaf*, which is also outstanding from the point of view of typography. Mr. Kenner is Jewish. In recognition of his devotion to the cause of his deaf coreligionists, the latter had made him a magnificent and most useful gift that honored the donors as much as the recipient.

E. Souweine

Leaving the print shop Mr. Kenner took us by a side street to another building and we went up to the fourth floor. On the huge landing, there were a number of office doors. The office of my old friend, Souweine, whom I had first met in 1893, was spacious and bathed in light. In reality, it was an engraver's studio. A charming young woman, the daughter of deaf parents in Brooklyn, was at the desk, next to a telephone. She was prompt to serve as interpreter for visitors and to take and make telephone calls. Almost all the deaf businessmen whom we met had a young woman to look after the telephone, and perform secretarial and bookkeeping duties. Nothing could be more practical.

Mr. Souweine does not work alone. He has two associates, Messrs. Ashes and Guglielmi, who have their own specialties and mostly work on their own. Orders are regular, abundant, especially in winter. The numerous samples that were on display or that we were shown in their boxes were all perfectly executed and printed. Mr. Souweine has a faithful clientele of long standing.

The Lexington Institution

So called in familiar terms because it is located at 901–922 Lexington Avenue. Others call it the Jewish Institution. In reality, when it was founded almost fifty-one years ago (1869) it had no denominational affiliation. Its objectives were purely and simply to inspire American educators of the deaf to adopt the German method. Here we have the third part of its articles of incorporation: "To introduce the articulation method of instructing deaf-mutes as practiced in Germany, by the establishment of an institution based on the eclectic system."

The eclectic system! This is at odds with the pure oral method, which admits of no other method than its own: speech and lipreading and nothing else. The Combined System, the mixture of methodologies that is the true eclectic system. Otherwise, words will have lost their meanings. But let us continue.

The true name is the Institution for the Improved Instruction of Deaf-Mutes. And indeed the school has made a great contribution to advance the education of the deaf. It has trained a number of quite remarkable deaf persons, even some who were not Jewish and had very limited competence in speech. Its great merit, as with the Houdin, Hugentobler, and Magnat schools in France in the past, is to show the possibility of teaching the deaf to speak.

At the beginning there were administrators, teachers, and pupils belonging to all religions. If Jewish pupils were in a majority, it was perhaps that their parents, coming from all the German-speaking regions, were more easily attracted to a method that had a similar origin. But the increase in the number of Jewish pupils created difficulties. In 1906, the New York City Council, at the urging of prominent Catholics, passed a bylaw that obliged the welfare offices, which were responsible along with the education office for the placement of children from poor families, to direct deaf youngsters to schools that were organized along religious lines. Protestants were to go to the Fort Washington school, Catholics to the Saint Joseph school in Fordham, and Jews to the school on Lexington Avenue. As a result the school's finances quickly went into the red. Then, in 1909 the institution more formally assumed a Jewish character and sought the support of Jewish authorities. Rabbi H. Pereira Mendes lent his active and powerful support; the Jewish community began to take an interest in the school, and raised a maintenance fund of $30,000. Other generous Jewish philanthropists supported the school with annual donations. In addition, pupil room and board fees brought in nearly $84,000. Revenues for 1915, the last year for which I received information, were $98,474.58 and expenses $97,780.42. The school's future then seems assured under such prudent and wise administration.

We went to visit one morning, Pilet, Graff, and I. The principal, Mr. Harris Taylor, was not there, nor, of course, were the pupils. Everyone was on their summer holidays! But the assistant matron, the gracious Miss Florence M. Hess, did the honors of the establishment. Everything was orderly and clean, bright and comfortable, with modern school furniture, shower stalls, and sinks of the latest hygienic design. Only the playgrounds dominated by the high walls of neighboring buildings seemed a little narrow, although they were in fact quite wide. More space would be desirable. But since this is the only special school in New York that is actually in the city, there is really no alternative.

In 1915 the number of pupils was 133 boys and 112 girls for a total of 245, of which 116 were supported by the state of New York and 115 by the city.

In addition to the principal, there were thirty-one male and female teachers. In the way of vocational instruction there was only dressmaking, sewing, embroidery, and cooking for girls, cabinet-making, tailoring, and drafting for boys. Other pupils learned trades in the city after they had completed their studies. And this is the best system.

One feature worth noting is that the institution retains the services of a consulting physician, a resident doctor, plus professionals in audiology, surgery, dermatology, oral surgery, ophthalmology, neurology, and dentistry.

James Constantin

Learning from Jacques Alexander that we were staying another week in New York, Mr. James Constantin invited us to dinner in Brooklyn.

This gave us an opportunity for a close look at the domestic life of New York workers. Mr. Constantin is a compositor with the same printing company where Mr. Alexander is employed as a draftsman. His home was on the fourth floor of a large apartment block. There were four or five rooms, but the whole apartment was rather cramped. The interior was furnished with taste by Mrs. Constantin, a distinguished speaking deaf woman, just like her kind sister, Dorothee Norbitt. Mrs. Constantin had prepared a good and plentiful dinner for us.

But the heat was overwhelming. We poured down vast quantities of beer or ice water. Once dinner was over, we went up on the roof. Here the roofs are flat, or have a slight pitch so that the rain runs off. There was no railing along the edges. That made us concerned for the charming little boy of the household. And just a few feet away the cars of the elevated railroad went by. During the hottest part of the summer the residents go up on the narrow roofs to get some air and usually gather around the chimney that serves their apartment. And because there are no railings, the residents of neighboring buildings can come and visit. This was how we made the acquaintance of Mr. and Mrs. Adler, an intelligent deaf couple who lived close by. The husband worked in a factory manufacturing gasoline tanks belonging to the famous Rockefeller brand.

We spent a very pleasant evening in the light breeze under a sky full of stars. Active in the Frats and Knights, Mr. Constantin was able to give us some very interesting information. His sister-in-law, Dorothee, told us that she worked in the Waterman fountain pen factory and that she was well paid. Just one more proof that the American deaf are capable of earning their own living.

JERSEY CITY
A Self-Made Man

The Garage of the Deaf Mechanic Ernst

In the subway on our return from Hartford we met a charming young couple who were also on their way home. The husband offered us his business card on which we saw that he was the owner of a garage. He asked us to come and visit him.

One morning, Graff and I decided to cross the Hudson and visit Jersey City, which is very close to New York City and is an industrial city with about 100,000 inhabitants. We would do our best to find our way to Mr. Ernst's garage.

It was a day of unbelievable heat. The ten-minute trip by ferry across the river scarcely gave us time to be refreshed by the light breeze. When we disembarked on the quay, there were several streetcar lines available to our uninformed choice. We took a car with a name on the plate that suggested it went to the end of the line on the far side of the city. This proved to be the case but the trip was a long one, through the animated city center, through neighborhoods of bungalows set among lawns, an area with factories, finally, sitting among vacant lots, we found a mysterious factory with a sign warning us not to approach. The driver and conductor of the streetcar looked at us and whispered between themselves while we looked around. Did they think we were spies?

We got back on the streetcar, which was getting ready to return, since we had more important things to do. As much to dismiss any suspicions he might have as to get the information we needed, I wrote a note to the conductor telling him that we were French and asking him whether the address Ernst had given us was somewhere along the line, and if it was, to tell us when to get off. He gave a sort of relieved nod with his head and very kindly made a sign to us to wait. Soon back in the center of the city, he signaled to us with a gesture and gave us a piece of paper on which he had sketched the route to follow. A few steps to the left, then straight ahead, then a turn to the left. We cast our eyes over the shop signs and right there on the corner we discovered that of the garage.

It was a huge hall, wide and deep, filled with automobiles of all makes and sizes, with empty spaces from which vehicles had been driven off. At the rear there was a forge and huge vises for repairs. One floor up there was a workshop with three rows of workbenches under sets of pulleys and gears.

Mr. Ernst came up to us, a good-humored, solid, and strongly built young man. He was in charge of the whole operation. He knew how to speak and could read lips. When necessary, he would write things out with pencil and paper. He had workmen under his supervision and a secretary to look after the telephone and typing. At the beginning he had been in business with his hearing brother. But the latter did not work hard enough and spent too much, so the deaf mechanic set up on his own. Since then, he said, business had been much better. In addition, Ernst had inherited some things from his father, who had died at an advanced age. He showed us his father's well used tools and some inventions that he had made to simplify the work. To fill out the work of the garage, Ernst got orders from a large factory nearby to make repairs or manufacture wrenches. Since his wife was on holiday at her parents, Ernst invited us to lunch in a restaurant.

After lunch, we got a better idea of what a self-made man he was and of his professional skill. Men from a delivery company brought in a coughing truck that refused to run. Through speech and lipreading Ernst discussed matters with them. The customers claimed that the problem lay with some part or other of the motor. Ernst looked, felt around, raised the hood, and applied his expert eye, then, smiling he pointed out the real cause of the malfunctioning to the astonished drivers. After that, he calmly drew up an estimate for the repair work, which would be considerable and would take the rest of the afternoon.

As we didn't want to keep him from his work, we said goodbye and told him how much we admired his achievement and what a fine example it would be to other deaf people who wanted to go into business for themselves. Curiously, a New Jersey state law prevents the deaf from driving automobiles, but Ernst said that he had an exemption from the police with whom he was on good terms.

He had advised us for our trip back to New York City to go on foot for about half an hour, along a street lined with plants and a soap factory that gave off odors like they were engaged in embalming cadavers. Then, just as we were in the middle of the street, a violent thunderstorm broke out, bringing torrents of warm rain. We succeeded in finding shelter in a bar, in front of some draughts of excellent, fresh, comforting beer. But back in New York they said that not a drop of rain had fallen, yet the two cities are separated only by the river. It was like coming back from the South Seas.

On Board the
Transatlantic Steamships
The Glorious Future

Among the Passengers and a Deaf Black Stoker

There are interesting things to be said about the life the delegates led aboard ship, especially in a time of war and with the risk of submarines, but this is beyond our subject. What is more relevant and noteworthy is the behavior of the deaf with the hearing passengers. I hasten to say that on our way to America and on our way home, the four of us were the objects of general sympathy and good will. We traveled in second class. The General Transatlantic Steamship Company had given us a discount. Its agents, both on board ship and in New York, were extremely obliging toward us. Here, we can renew our thanks to Mr. J. Dal Piaz, the eminent director of the company, who remembered that one of the former presidents of the company, M. Eugene Pereire, had always been a supporter of the deaf, in memory of his grandfather, Rodriguez Pereire, who had been one of the first French educators of the deaf, at the same time as the Abbé de l'Épée.

The passengers, French and American, Italian and Spanish, and even a Serbian delegate, Mr. Jovanovic, enjoyed talking with us, either by writing in French or English or in the case of some few by using the finger alphabet, which they knew. There were even two French passengers who wanted M. Graff to teach it to them. On the return trip, the steamship had many more American soldiers than civilian passengers, in addition to YMCA volunteers. And a number of these, including some charming young women, came to chat with us through the medium of the manual alphabet.

As can be seen, the manual alphabet is a great aid to relations between the hearing and the deaf. Wider general knowledge of it would be a great benefit for both parties but in particular for the deaf.

On the ship bound for Europe there was also a medical celebrity, Dr. Carrle, whose far-reaching discoveries were known to everyone. He noted the French foursome, came up to us and engaged in a written conversation. He asked us which method was better suited to the education of the deaf, the French or American one. As this report clearly shows, the present American method is certainly to be preferred. But it is a method of French origin, while the official French method of the day is German in origin!

On our way to America, one of the ship's crew remarked to us that among the black stokers there was one who was deaf. We asked him to point the deaf stoker out to us. He was a big fellow from Senegal, intelligent and sturdy, but he could make himself understood only by means of his own impromptu signs. He was married but his wife had left him. As in the case of certain white women, she could not tolerate the fact that he was deaf. His foreman told us that the man had been inconsolable ever since. But he was a conscientious worker who forgot his misfortunes in the execution of his duties.

On our way home among the distractions on board, mostly devised by the Americans, were Swedish calisthenics. Twice a day, the soldiers and some of the civilians went to it with enthusiasm. Two of our party, Gaillard and Graff, joined them. These limbering up exercises stretched their bodies, strengthened their

lungs with the help of the fresh sea air, and toned up their mus-
cles. Even in the submarine danger zone, these group calisthenics were continued, showing our unconcern for the vain threats
of the enemy and our confidence in the glorious future of France,
the United States, and their allies, once peace had been restored.

APPENDIX
Speech by M. Edwin A. Hodgson

Benefits of Education to the Deaf

We celebrate today one hundred years of educational opportunity for the deaf. We render homage to the great, the good, the benevolent Thomas Hopkins Gallaudet, to whose wisdom and philanthropy our emancipation from the thralldom of ignorance is due.

Antecedent to that memorable morning of April 15, 1817, when the first school for the deaf in the New World was opened, thousands had lived and died in mental darkness. The native intelligence existed, but there were no systematic attempts to cultivate and develop it. The imprisoned soul yearned in vain for inspiration from the people, the books, the culture that cried out to it on every hand.

> For knowledge to their eyes her ample
> page,
> Rich with the spoils of time, did n'er
> unroll;

Stark helplessness repressed their noble
    rage,
And from the genial current of the soul.

We have been told, year after year, on the recurrence of Gallaudet's birth—the tenth of December—the story of his life. His ancestry can be traced back to Joshua Gallaudet, who lived in the little village of Mauze, near La Rochelle, in France, at the time of the Edict of Nantes, in 1685. Joshua Gallaudet was married to Margaret Prioleauy, the granddaughter of Elizée Prioleau, a distinguished Huguenot minister. To Joshua and Margaret Gallaudet was born a son, Peter Elisha, a physician, who fled, shortly after the Revocation, to New Rochelle, N.Y. He married, and had a son, Thomas, who was born in 1724. Thomas married Catherine Edgar, and their second son, Peter Wallace, married Jane Hopkins of Hartford, Conn. She was a descendant of John Hopkins, one of the Puritan settlers of Hartford. On December 10, 1787, a son was born to Peter Wallace and Jane Gallaudet, Thomas Hopkins Gallaudet, the one we are assembled here today to honor.

The parents of Thomas Hopkins Gallaudet moved to Philadelphia when he was thirteen years of age. In the autumn of 1802, Gallaudet entered Yale College, qualifying for the sophomore class. In a class of forty-two, he was one of six who graduated with the honor of an oration. He later took a course at Andover Theological Seminary, graduating in 1814.

I am warned that other speakers will discourse on Gallaudet's life in a more exhaustive vein, so this brief statement is merely to show that, by heredity, environment, and the trend of his education, Gallaudet was favorably influenced and fittingly prepared for the noble part he played in the philanthropies and charities which distinguished his career.

You are all familiar with Gallaudet's journey across the Atlantic in search of information concerning the methods of instructing the deaf that had been pursued in England, Scotland, and France. How he was rebuffed and refused assistance in Great

Britain, and eventually aided by the Abbé Sicard, who had succeeded de l'Épée in France. And, finally, his return to America in August, 1816, bringing not only a knowledge of the French system of educating the deaf, but also a brilliant exponent of that system in the person of Laurent Clerc.

Gallaudet and Clerc traveled from city to city, giving expositions, which brought money and friends to the cause of the education of the deaf. In fact, Gallaudet demonstrated to the people what we are still trying to show them today—that the deaf and dumb can be educated up to a very high degree of proficiency, and become active, earnest, honest, and capable citizens of the state.

And so the first school for the deaf in America was born of benevolence. It was dependent upon charity. Its founder was confronted with public skepticism and private indifference, and the road to success seemed both difficult and doubtful. But the strength of will, the nobility of purpose, the unwavering faith of Gallaudet in the righteousness of the cause he espoused, conquered all opposition and ultimate victory was won. God's sunlight shone upon the deaf and dumb.

There were seven pupils in the first class that assembled at Hartford, when the education of the deaf was begun, on April 15, 1817. They were Alice Cogswell, George Loring, Wilson Whiton, Abigail Dillingham, Otis Waters, John Brewster, and Nancy Orr. Three of them became teachers (George Loring, Wilson Whiton, and Abigail Dillingham). John Brewster, who entered at the age of fifty-one years, is chronicled as a portrait painter.

Levi H. Backus, who is tenth on the list of pupils who entered in 1817, after a course of five years, taught at a private school for the deaf in Canajoharie, N.Y., and became editor of the Canajoharie *Radii*, in which he conducted one or more columns of deaf-mute news, in the year 1839 or thereabouts. He was the pioneer in deaf–mute journalism in this country. He obtained a small subsidy from the state. Later on, aided by this same legislative grant, Henry C. Rider founded and conducted the *Deaf Mutes' Journal* from the year 1872 to 1879, since which time it has been my especial honor and pride to have been its editor, although no state subsidy has been claimed or received for a quarter of a century.

Less than a month after the opening of the "Connecticut Asylum for the Education and Instruction of Deaf and Dumb Persons," as the school was then officially designated, there entered a young lady pupil, who was destined to give a tremendous impulse to the uplift of the deaf. She was Sophia Fowler, of Guilford, Conn., and, at the date of admission, May 7, 1817, she was a comely and intelligent young lady of nineteen years. Her native mentality was so bright, her diligence and studious disposition so marked, that in a course of four years her progress was remarkably rapid, and this, combined with her personal charms and loveliness of character, won the heart of her teacher, and she became Mrs. Thomas Hopkins Gallaudet. She was the mother of Dr. Edward Miner Gallaudet and Rev. Dr. Thomas Gallaudet, the first of whom founded the only college for the higher education of the deaf; the other the first church for the deaf, the first home for aged and infirm deaf–mutes, and also established religious missions that at present are actively engaged in promoting the welfare of the deaf in nearly every state in the Union.

Taking into consideration the meager educational facilities and the inadequate provisions for instructing the deaf in the infant years of the first school, coupled with the advanced ages and short terms of the pupils, one is amazed at the wonderful results attained. Shall we credit it to the teachers, or to the extraordinary native talent of the pupils? Or was it because of the broad, free, and untrammeled use of the sign language, which was the basis of the French system employed?

Since the advantages of education have come to them, the great majority of the deaf have lived lives of useful and intelligent industry. They have proved themselves productive factors in the wealth and welfare of the community and loyal citizens of the state. Their careers have formed examples of courage and zeal in overcoming obstacles that the condition of deafness has placed in their pathways, for they have been alert and ready to render a full meed of service in every occupation that has engaged the capabilities of their heads and hands.

Of those who derived their intellectual sustenance at Hartford within the first half century of its existence, and made exceptional records for mental culture, force of character and professional accomplishment, particular mention might be made of the following.

William Willard, founder of the Indiana Institution, for two years its principal, and, subsequently, for twenty years a valued instructor.

Edmund Booth, a giant in stature as well as in intellect, who, for a few years, was a teacher at his alma mater. He removed to Iowa, where he published and edited the Auamosa *Eureka*, a newspaper for the hearing community. He also held public office in that city for many years.

Job Turner, who was a teacher in Virginia, and for nearly thirty years an ordained minister of the Episcopal Church, with a mission field that covered every locality south of the Mason and Dixon line.

William B. Swett, who founded the New England Industrial School at Beverly, Mass., and conducted it with great success until his death.

William Martin Chamberlain, teacher, editor, and remarkable man in public affairs.

George A. Holmes, whose influence and activities helped to consolidate the interests of the deaf of New England, in religious and organized enterprise.

James Denison, for nearly three decades was principal of Kendall School. He was the inventor of the Denison

Fraction Scale, a contrivance for teaching fractions. As a writer of prose he was graceful in expression and forceful in presentation. He also was a writer of poetry of more than ordinary merit.

Melville Ballard was the first graduate of Gallaudet College. For many years he was an instructor at Kendall School. He attained superiority in the French language, and was a leading example of the successful work of the Combined System.

H. Humphrey Moore, one of the really great artists in oils, whose canvasses, remarkable for coloring, composition and originality, may be seen in many of the art institutes and public and private galleries of this and other countries.

Philip A. Emery founded the Kansas Institution and also the Chicago day schools. For a few years he was principal of the Kansas Institution and for many years presided over and guided the day schools in Chicago.

Fisher Ames Spofford, who became an instructor of deaf children at the institution in Columbus, Ohio.

T. Green, a polished and scholarly gentleman, who introduced American methods into the institution for the deaf in Belleville, Ontario, Canada, and was a teacher there until his death.

Joseph G. Parkinson, at one time Chief Examiner of Patents in the United States Patent Office, and during his later years a patent attorney in Chicago.

William L. Hill, proprietor and editor of the most influential newspaper in his section, the Athol, Mass., *Transcript*.

Henry C. White founded two institutions for the education of the deaf, the Utah Institution at Ogden and the Arizona Institution at Phoenix. He is also a compiler of a book on common law.

A close scrutiny of the early records of the Hartford School will reveal many others who carved so well their path in the world as to reflect credit on their alma mater.

Linking the first half century of education for the deaf with the second, are such distinguished products of our schools as

John Carlin, a miniature painter, a classical scholar, a poet, and a painter of biblical and historical studies.

Albert Newsam, the greatest lithographer and engraver of his time.

And these preceptors and exemplars of the benefits of education to the deaf and dumb: Walter W. Angus and Sidney J. Vail, of Indiana; Zachariah McCoy, of Wisconsin; William M. L. Bregg and Thomas L. Brown, of Michigan; Selah Wait, of Illinois; Miss Ida Montgomery, of New York; Thomas Jefferson Trist, of Philadelphia. And it would be almost criminal to forget "Old Tom" Brown, of New Hampshire, who, in 1871 like Cincinnatus of old, left his plow to organize the deaf, at Albany, N.Y., and lead the movement to perpetuate with a monument the memory of the first deaf-mute teacher in America, Laurent Clerc.

There was one school for the deaf on the American continent on April 1817, and seven pupils under instruction. Today there are 157 schools in the United States, sixty-four of which are public residential schools, seventy-four public day schools, and nineteen denominational and private schools. The aggregate number of pupils is quite close onto fifteen thousand, and the total annual expenditure for their education is approximately three and a half million dollars.

The little seed that Gallaudet planted at Hartford became a tree of enlightenment, which has burgeoned and grown and expanded until its overspreading branches encompass a continent, wherein the boon and blessing of an education to every deaf child no longer depends upon sporadic charity or private opulence, but is vested in the economic wisdom and careful liberality of the state.

The progressive spread of the elementary schools was fast providing for the educational welfare of the deaf of the nation. In the year 1864 there were twenty-six institutions for instructing the deaf in the ordinary branches of a common school course. Still there were many deaf mutes possessed of the mental capacity and imbued with the worthy aspiration to pursue an advanced curriculum. Therefore, the crowning triumph of the education of the deaf was signalized by the establishment of the National Deaf-Mute College (now Gallaudet College) at Kendall Green, Washington, D.C. Its founder was Edward Miner Gallaudet, Ph.D., LL.D., who, valiantly bearing the burden of fourscore years, is with us today.

Gallaudet College is the only college for the deaf in the world, and its founder is universally regarded as the highest living authority upon the education of the deaf. To Gallaudet College deaf men have come from different countries to secure the benefits of a higher education, which could not be obtained in their own countries. About thirty years ago its doors were opened to young ladies, and since then the work of coeducation has been carried forward with commendable success. A large percentage of the leading deaf of the United States received their intellectual polish at Kendall Green. Another valuable function of Gallaudet College is the "Normal Course" of one year, offered to graduates of universities, colleges, and high schools, who aspire to become teachers of the deaf. Many men and not a few women, who have attained distinction in the profession of teaching, were trained for the work in Gallaudet's Normal Courses.

Since the college was established, its influence upon the education of the deaf has been steady and cumulative. The standards of the various institutions have been repeatedly raised in order to enable prospective students to meet the requirements of the college entrance examinations. It is the glowing jewel in the diadem of education in which the wide circle of institutions form the surrounding cluster.

The benefits the deaf have derived from the special schools for their education is evidenced by their home life, by their status in society, in the marts of industry, and in the political community.

They pursue with skill and ability almost every occupation in which the sense of hearing is not absolutely essential. The percentage of incompetents is so low as to be almost negligible. There are many instances in which inherent genius and native talent have been developed to an extraordinary degree and produced success in the higher avocations. As a matter of historical record, it seems fitting to chronicle herein a few of those who have risen superior to the ordinary lines of employment and reached out to better things.

First of all, I would mention Douglas Tilden, whose creations in sculpture and other accomplishments, stamp him as the greatest living deaf-mute. An artist in oils, a caricaturist, a writer of English that is forceful, cynical, euphonious, and poetical as he wills, he stands before the world as a rare and versatile genius.

The late Rev. Henry Winter Syle, with gentle ways and an indomitable force of character, was the first deaf-mute in the history of Christianity to break through the red tape of ecclesiasticism and become an ordained minister of the Gospel. He was a scholar of eminence, a chemist and assayer of high standing, and a friend and companion of both the high and humble deaf, for whom he incessantly labored and eventually gave his life.

In analytical and synthetical chemistry we have superior exponents in George T. Dougherty of Chicago; Isaac Goldberg of Brooklyn; James W. Howson of Berkeley; David Friedman of Cleveland.

Dudley Webster George, a teacher at the Illinois institution, has polyglot proclivities to such an extent that he has mastered half a dozen modern languages.

In architecture, Olof Hanson of Washington State; S. Marr of Tennessee; A. O. Steidemann of Missouri; Charles W. Fetscher of New York.

Gerald McCarthy despite the double handicap of deafness and poor eyesight became State Botanist for South Carolina.

Jay Cooke Howard, of Duluth, Minn., is a banker and real estate man of enviable reputation; and Samuel Frankenheim, of New York, as a broker and financier has made his mark.

James H. Logan, of Pittsburgh, Penn., has been a United States Government Microscopist, and Demonstrator of Microscopy at the Western Pennsylvania Medical College. He is also the compiler of that wonderful collection of simplified stories published under the title of *The Raindrop*.

Strange as it may seem, the deaf have in not a few instances developed poetical talent. Some of them have published volumes of poetry that competent critics concede to possess real merit. In the galaxy of deaf poets the following may be enumerated: John Carlin, Mrs. Mary Toles Peet, Mrs. Laura C. R. Searing, Miss Alice R. Jennings, Mrs. Angie Fuller Fischer, Mrs. May Martin Stafford, J. Schuyler Long, Frederick J. Meagher, J. W. Sowell, J. H. McFarlane, Howard L. Terry.

The late Robert H. King was a notary public and insurance agent, and at the time of his death was Director of the Kentucky Institution. Notwithstanding his deafness, he served in the Union with distinction during the Civil War.

Frank R. Gray is a skilled maker of optical and scientific instruments, and an amateur astronomer of no small caliber.

Cadwallader Washburn, of Minnesota, won fame as an etcher, and also as an artist in oils and watercolors. Granville Redmond, of California, and Will Quinlan, of

New York, have both worked their way to distinction with the brush and palette. Albert Ballin, Jacques Alexander, and Miss Ruby Abrams, of New York, are also artists deserving of mention. Elmer R. Hannan, of Washington, D. C., although he has not created a chef d'oeuvre as a sculptor, has been successful in producing work of considerable merit.

A. R. Spear, of Minnesota, founder of the North Dakota Institution for the Deaf, and for five years its superintendent, is patentee of a merchandise mailing envelope. It is made in his own factory, and extensively sold in wholesale quantities.

Anton Schroeder, another Minnesotan, is an inventor and manufacturer of storm-sash and doorscreen hangers.

George W. Veditz is a fluent writer in English, French, and German, and a prolific contributor to magazines and newspapers. He is also the "poultry king" of Colorado. At chess he is the only man to have vanquished a national champion.

The late James E. Gallaher was principal of the Chicago Day Schools, a splendid writer, an ardent worker, a deep thinker, and an author of valuable books relating to the deaf.

Leo C. Williams, of San Francisco, a man of unquestionable grit and enterprise, has made a fortune as a contractor in big business that required skill along engineering lines.

William W. Beadell has successfully edited newspapers for the hearing community in Illinois and Vermont, and for the past fifteen years has been editor and proprietor of the Arlington, N.J., *Observer*.

Alexander L. Pach, of New York, was for many years head of the printing department of Pach Bros., Photographers on Fifth Avenue. He also had charge of the purchasing, publicity, correspondence and auditing of the firm's extensive business. At the age of fifty, he started a studio of his own, on Broadway facing Wall Street. In three years he has made a wonderful record for success, and at this writing is filling a contract for photographing 1,300 officials of a big financial establishment, which calls for forty sitters on each working day. His studio has every modern facility, is luxuriously appointed, and includes three assistants and a busy stenographer.

Frank P. Gibson, by his wonderful power as an organizer, has made the National Fraternal Society of the Deaf the greatest and most prosperous mutual insurance organization of the deaf that the world has ever known.

Dr. Edwin Nies has a lucrative practice in dentistry, and also is instructor in oral hygiene at the Vanderbilt Clinic in New York City.

In New York City, Emanuel Souweine has been a boss engraver for twenty years; William Rose is proprietor of an extensive printing business; Edward Elsworth owns a fine printing plant, including a linotype; and each of them employs both deaf and hearing experts in the lines they represent.

The profession of teaching has enlisted the energies of a considerable number of deaf men and women—men and women of erudite scholarship and specialized skill in the art of teaching—whose absorbing ambition has been, and is at the present day, to cultivate the intellect and develop the native talent of the "silent children" entrusted to their care. There are very few instances indeed in which deaf teachers have failed to make good, for their sympathies, their very souls, are lured into the task by some mysterious power that lends them aid and inspiration. Some of these deaf teachers have, by mental superiority and

forceful personality, eclipsed and outranked in position not a few
of their colleagues who can hear. Shining on this roster are Dr.
John B. Hotchkiss and Dr. Amos G. Draper, professors at Gallaudet College; Dr. Robert Patterson, principal of the Ohio Institution; Dr. Thomas Francis Fox, senior assistant, in the academic
department, to the principal of the New York Institution; Rev.
Dr. James H. Cloud, Principal of the St. Louis Day School for
the Deaf; Dr. James L. Smith, head teacher at the Minnesota
Institution; the late May Martin Stafford, who was a professor
of English at Gallaudet College; Dr. Samuel Gaston Davidson,
late of the Philadelphia Institution, but at present conducting a
private school for the deaf in New Hampshire; Prof. James M.
Stewart, supervisor and principal of the Manual Department of
the Michigan Institution; Dr. J. Schuyler Long, principal of the
Iowa Institution; Jonathan Holbrook Eddy, head teacher in the
Arkansas Institution; Dr. Warren Robinson, of the Wisconsin
Institution; and professors like Robert P. McGregor and Augustus B. Greener of Ohio, George M. McClure of Kentucky,
William George Jones of New York, George Moredock Teegar-
den of Pennsylvania, Albert Berg of Indiana, Arthur L. Roberts
of Kansas, J. H. McFarlane of Alabama, J. W. Sowell of Nebraska,
Theophilus d'Estrella and Winfield S. Runde of California, John
E. Crane of Hartford, etc.

Religious instruction had an important place in the curriculum of the Hartford School from the moment it was founded,
and in fact the inculcation of religious duty and scriptural knowledge has ever been a recognized responsibility in all the institutions for instructing the deaf that have subsequently been
established. Therefore, it seems strange that thirty-five years had
elapsed before the offices of the church were brought to the adult
deaf and dumb.

Rev. Dr. Thomas Gallaudet, son of the founder of deaf-mute
education, and a brother of the founder of Gallaudet College, was
the first to inaugurate this special mission in the year 1850. In 1852
he founded St. Ann's Church for Deaf mutes, and in 1872 he
organized the Church Mission to Deaf mutes, which brought the

comforts of religion at specified periods to the populous centers of a field that embraced nearly all the states east of the Rocky Mountains. This mission, through the benevolence of its founder, also provided a Home for Aged and Infirm Deaf. St. Ann's Church for Deaf mutes rejoices in an exclusive edifice for the deaf, wherein on each Sunday of the year, and on the Holy Days of the church calendar, the gospel of Christ crucified is preached to silent congregations. It has besides a parish house well equipped for mental improvement, charitable work, and social recreation. The Home for Aged and Infirm Deaf is a splendid fireproof building, which shelters on an average twenty-six aged and infirm deaf–mutes of both sexes. It is situated midway between New Hamburg and Poughkeepsie, on a site overlooking the Hudson River, and comprises a farm of one hundred and fifty–six acres. Through legacies and voluntary contributions this institution has acquired an endowment fund of nearly two hundred thousand dollars.

At present there are fifteen clergymen of the Episcopal faith ministering exclusively to the deaf, all but one of whom are deaf. It is the glory of the Episcopal Church that she first opened her doors to the deaf and ordained them. The first deaf-mute minister, Rev. Henry Winter Syle, and Revs. Austin W. Mann and Job Turner, have gone to their reward. Rev. John H. Keiser is associated with Rev. Dr. John Chamberlain, in the dioceses of New York, Long Island, and Newark.

Rev. Charles Orvis Dantzer is pastor of All Souls' Church in Philadelphia, with missions in Trenton, N.J., Delaware, and Maryland.

Rev. Oliver J. Whildin prosecutes his work within the confines of the city of Baltimore.

Rev. Harry Van Allen officiates in the dioceses of Albany and western New York.

Rev. Brewster R. Allabough is in charge of the Mid-Western Deaf-Mute Mission, a large and important mission field covering several states. He succeeded the late Rev. Austin Ward Mann, who planned this missionary district.

Rev. Franklin C. Smielau has an extensive field in central Pennsylvania.

Rev. George F. Flick is pastor of All Souls' Church for the Deaf, in Chicago, and also holds services in Minnesota and Wisconsin.

Rev. Jacob M. Koehler has a large territory in the trans-Mississippi district.

Rev. George H. Hefflon is a faithful apostle of the master in New England.

Rev. Herbert C. Merrill serves in Washington, D. C., and the South.

Rev. H. Lorraine Tracy in Louisiana and the Gulf states. Rev. Clarence W. Charles, recently ordained, has as yet no specified field.

Rev. Clarence Webb officiates in the Diocese of Los Angeles.

The Methodists have a well–established mission in Chicago, in the charge of Rev. Dr. Philip J. Hasenstab.

Christ Methodist Episcopal Church for the Deaf in Baltimore is in the charge of Rev. Daniel Moylan.

Rev. R. Clayton Wyand is another Marylander who has conducted missions and preaches under the authority of the Baptists.

Rev. John W. Michaels is a Baptist Evangelist in the southern states.

The Presbyterians are established in western Pennsylvania and other places.

Of late years the Lutherans have been very active. They have chapels in Chicago, Milwaukee, Minneapolis, and Detroit, and missions in New York, St. Louis, Kansas City, Los Angeles, and Seattle.

For over thirty-five years the priests of the Roman Catholic Church have ministered to the spiritual welfare of the deaf men and women who belong by heritage to the mother church. They have established missions in New York, Boston, Baltimore, Philadelphia, Chicago, St. Paul, and other places. Societies with benevolent and social aims are favored with assistance and encouragement.

The Hebrews have organized congregations in New York, Philadelphia, and Boston, and are conducting an intensive campaign for the deaf of that faith. The New York Communal Center is in the charge of Rabbi Amateau. It includes a clubhouse for social recreation, and affords facilities for the prosecution of other work of eleemosynary character.

To religious organization must be ascribed the impulse to provide for the aged and the infirm, following the lead of Rev. Dr. Thomas Gallaudet, who in 1872 founded the Gallaudet home, just twenty years after he founded St. Ann's Church for Deaf mutes. The deaf did their share in providing the initial fund needed and helped in the cost of maintenance.

Other homes for the aged and infirm are the Pennsylvania home at Doylestown, the Ohio home at Westerville, the New England home at Everett, Mass. All of them were established through the agency of organizations of the deaf. In the states of Illinois and Indiana, respectively, the funds have reached a point where the erection of buildings is being contemplated. The Indiana home project owes its inception to the benevolence of Mr. Orson Archibald, a deaf-mute who made a munificent gift of land for the purpose.

The first secular organization of adult deaf–mutes in the United States of which there is any record, was the "Gallaudet Monument Association," effected in 1851, shortly after the elder Gallaudet's death. Its sole object was to erect a monument to their first great friend and benefactor. Laurent Clerc was made president of the association, and in 1854, the object being accomplished, the association ceased to exist.

In the year 1871 at Albany, N.Y., the first association national in constituency was organized, with Thomas Brown, of Henniker, N.H., as president. This association also had for its object the outward expression of gratitude for benefits bestowed, which took the form of a monument in memory of Laurent Clerc. This monument was unveiled with appropriate ceremonials in 1874, stands but a few yards distant from the Gallaudet monument in front of the American School.

It might be correct to say that the New England Gallaudet Association, which draws its members from the six New England states, is a continuation of the association that erected the Clerc monument in 1874.

These pioneers of united effort were the focus of attention in their day. But the increase of education has wrought wonderful changes, and now associations of the deaf exist as customary and progressive fixtures in nearly every state of the Union. The schools have their literary societies, in which pupils become accustomed to interchange of opinion, familiar with parliamentary usage, and acquire an easy and collected manner of address in the presence of large audiences. Therefore, when school days are over, the transition to adult societies, clubs, or associations, is a natural affiliation begotten of intelligent interest.

Apart from the state and alumni associations, there are two organizations that have claims on all the deaf everywhere. The first of these is the National Fraternal Society of the Deaf, which is an incorporated mutual insurance organization that has divisions in different states and different cities of the same state. It exists under the same legal privileges and restrictions as govern all other mutual benefit societies. It pays sick and death benefits, and has at the present time a fund of more than $135,000, with a membership aggregating 2,850 men, whose admission required them to pass a physical examination made by a physician.

The National Association of the Deaf, under the auspices of which most of us are gathered here today, was organized in Cincinnati in 1880, and incorporated under the laws of the District of Columbia in the year 1900. There is no direct benefit accruing to membership, as its purposes are altruistic. Its membership roll embraces the best educated, most forceful, and progressive deaf people of the entire country. Its objects are "the improvement, development and extension of Schools for the Deaf throughout the world, and especially in the United States; and the intellectual, professional and industrial improvement and the social enjoyment of the members." It has grown in power and influence, and the results of its deliberations go out to the people as the consensus of opinion of the leading deaf men and women in the civilized world.

The gratitude of the deaf to their benefactors in the educational world has found expression in various ways. As early as 1850, the deaf of New England and other states presented to Thomas Hopkins Gallaudet and to Laurent Clerc, each a massive silver pitcher and salver, made from silver coins contributed by the deaf only. And after the founder and the first teacher had passed to their reward, honored each with an imposing monument. In the year 1889, commemorating the centennial of Gallaudet's birth, the deaf of the nation placed a heroic statue of bronze on the terrace fronting Gallaudet College at Washington, D.C., representing our first benefactor teaching Alice Cogswell in the manual alphabet the letter "A."

The martyred president, James A. Garfield, a friend of the deaf and a patron of Gallaudet College, is commemorated by the deaf with a marble bust in the chapel of the college.

The Peets, father and son, are honored with bas-relief portraits in the New York Institution chapel, besides large oil portraits in the entrance hall, and the present principal, Enoch Henry Currier, has been the proud recipient of a splendid allegorical statue of bronze, a massive silver loving cup, and a magnificent saber, which testify to the love and esteem of the deaf.

The benevolent and self–sacrificing Rev. Dr. Thomas Gallaudet has his kindnesses and benefactions recorded on bronze tablets, at the church that he founded and at the home he established and which bears his name.

In the various state schools for the deaf there are many portraits in oil, that have been placed on the walls to demonstrate the love of the deaf and their grateful loyalty to their friends.

The various features of this paper have been touched upon all too lightly, because the time limit allowed me admits of no other course. I could multiply the living examples of high-standard successes, and still merit reproach for omitting others quite as worthy. Each of those mentioned acquired success through the advantages of education, and none of them owes advancement to the propulsive power of the plethoric purse. They are products of the Combined System of educating the deaf—a system that does not smother native talent nor quench the fires of a laudable ambition; a system that includes the utilization of every method of proven value; a system that does not standardize mentality, but is so adjusted and applied that every grade of intelligence is encouraged to grow and develop; a system that does not restrain the natural bent, except to direct the energies into proper channels; a system that neglects no single deaf child, but is assurance of a full measure of benefit to all. Is it any wonder that the best educated deaf are saturated with the conviction that "single–method" schools can not possibly fulfill to the utmost the educational functions which are the sole justification for their existence?

At the beginning of the nineteenth century, the deaf and dumb were classed with the unfit. In these early years of the twentieth century—one hundred years after Thomas Hopkins Gallaudet founded the first school for their benefit—the deaf live and labor on terms of equality with those who, by birth or accident, have not been deprived of any of the five senses. In these days of war, their patriotism cannot be doubted. Hundreds of them are hungering for the privilege of serving on the battle line. They are anxious either to fight with the gun and grenade in the trenches, or aid the sick and the wounded as stretcher-bearers, or in any other capacity under the merciful mission of the Red Cross. Even now there are a great many employed in munitions factories, and many more will this year wield the hoe on the farm to help the men behind the guns to quick and certain victory.

In New York City alone, the deaf have subscribed to the Liberty Loan, through a deaf-mute broker, in amounts aggregating more than $28,000, and this sum would be vastly increased if the subscriptions through banks could be added. In other parts of the United States, there can be little doubt but the deaf have done equally well.

That Thomas Hopkins Gallaudet founded the first school in America for the education of the deaf is sufficient in itself to make the name of Gallaudet a patronymic to be honored and revered for all time. But he did still more. He gave the life service of two talented sons—the eldest and the youngest—each of whom exerted a most puissant influence in the uplift of the deaf.

The youngest son of the family is Edward Miner Gallaudet Ph.D., LL.D. Unfettered by the cares and worries of the world he is peacefully passing the sunset of life amid scenes of his childhood, in Hartford, Conn. He it was who gave to the deaf the opportunity and privilege of a collegiate course where success is rewarded with the honor of a degree. Though his frame has been enfeebled by the stress and strain of nearly fourscore years of active life, he retains the lion heart and dominant spirit that characterized the days of his prime, and is still the astute diplomat and the courteous gentleman whom many generations of students at Gallaudet College admired and loved.

The eldest son, Rev. Thomas Gallaudet, D.D., L.H.D., died on the twenty-seventh day of August, 1902. He was a wonderful man intellectually, and could have become a pulpit orator of great honor and distinction. But he chose the benevolent path among the "children of silence." The Creator never placed on earth a man of kindlier heart and gentler ways. The emoluments of his sacred office were insignificant, but the good he accomplished is of permanent value and beyond computation. When he died the entire world of the deaf was saddened. He created for the benefit of future generations of the deaf well–organized mission fields, a home for the aged and infirm, and a church edifice exclusively for their use. It could truly be said of him, when passing from this world forever:

> He scarce had need to doff his pride or
>   slough the dross of earth,
> E'en as he trod that day to God, so
>   walked he from his birth,
> In simpleness and gentleness and honor
>   and clean mirth.
> So cup to lip, in fellowship, they gave
>   him welcome high,
> And made a plate at the banquet board,
>   the strong men ranged thereby,
> Who had done his work and held his
>   peace and did not fear to die.

For the benefits which education has conferred; for the inspiration and the happiness it has brought; for the useful and productive lives that we are enabled to lead; for the privilege of bearing the burdens of good citizenship, aiding the progress and sharing in the prosperity of the nation; for all these and other blessings, the love of grateful hearts goes out to the memory of our first great benefactor, Thomas Hopkins Gallaudet.

INDEX